# JAGUAR HEART

THE COURAGE TO FEEL,
THE COURAGE TO SEE,
THE NEED TO FORGIVE AND HEAL

*Anna Dodds*

One Printers Way
Altona, MB R0G 0B0
Canada

www.friesenpress.com

**Copyright © 2024 by Anna Dodds**
First Edition — 2024

All rights reserved.

No part of this publication may be reproduced in any form, or by any means, electronic or mechanical, including photocopying, recording, or any information browsing, storage, or retrieval system, without permission in writing from FriesenPress.

ISBN
978-1-03-830434-6 (Hardcover)
978-1-03-830433-9 (Paperback)
978-1-03-830435-3 (eBook)

1. BIOGRAPHY & AUTOBIOGRAPHY, PERSONAL MEMOIRS
2. RELIGION, SPIRITUALITY

Distributed to the trade by The Ingram Book Company

*This book is dedicated to all daughters
who have been victimized by their own mothers.
May they become aware of their own true essence
and the sacredness of their role as women in society.
May they be founders of empowered lineages.*

# Contents

| | |
|---|---|
| Preface | 1 |
| Introduction | 5 |
| **Part I: That's Life** | **7** |
| Chapter 1 | 9 |
| Chapter 2 | 17 |
| Chapter 3 | 27 |
| Chapter 4 | 37 |
| Chapter 5 | 43 |
| Chapter 6 | 51 |
| Chapter 7 | 61 |
| Chapter 8 | 69 |
| Chapter 9 | 75 |
| Chapter 10 | 87 |
| Chapter 11 | 95 |
| **PART II: The Other Side** | **99** |
| Chapter 12 | 101 |
| Chapter 13 | 107 |
| Chapter 14 | 115 |
| Chapter 15 | 123 |

| | |
|---|---|
| Chapter 16 | 129 |
| Chapter 17 | 133 |
| Chapter 18 | 141 |
| Chapter 19 | 147 |
| Chapter 20 | 153 |
| Chapter 21 | 161 |
| Chapter 22 | 167 |
| Chapter 23 | 175 |
| Chapter 24 | 187 |
| Chapter 25 | 195 |
| **PART III: Merging the Sides** | **201** |
| Chapter 26 | 203 |
| Chapter 27 | 211 |
| Chapter 28 | 219 |
| Chapter 29 | 227 |
| Chapter 30 | 233 |
| Acknowledgments | 237 |
| Bibliographical References | 239 |
| About the Author | 241 |

# *Preface*

Writing down the memories of my life has caused me much pain. As I say in the text of this book, my struggles with compositions and essays at school, the comments by teachers, and the lingering trauma about writing I endured from my mother had conditioned me to believe that I do not have a talent for writing and that I should hide my shortcoming by honing other skills. I hated writing all my life, or perhaps I should say that I was frightened by it. In addition, I was not inclined to read literary books. I did not read the great classics. I could not stand reading hundreds of pages and getting emotionally entangled in the author's eloquence and fantastic imagination.

What is more, I was adamant that I would never ever write the story of my life, as two close friends of mine did as an exercise along their spiritual path. I was so gripped by shame for all I had done and what happened to me that I would rather die than expose myself yet again to judgment and ridicule.

Nor was I convinced about the benefit of journaling as a therapeutic tool. A brief note would be quite enough for me, as brief as a thought, to be wrinkled up and tossed out as soon as it became obsolete in my feelings. Journaling would have been an effort, forcing the art that I do not have to make a thought prettier and longer, but in the end, diluting the meaning I wished to convey and fixing on paper the bad energy that I wished to be rid of.

But in my retirement, I have had the opportunity to let go of many energy impediments that jammed my soul. Retirement is a watershed that, if accepted, is a blessing. It has allowed me to rediscover activities that I had forgotten about. It has also presented me with new needs that sit well with both my age and personality—the personality that I had to disguise and keep in a waiting room within myself while I was engaged in social life, studying, and working.

Solitude has always represented the space where I could breathe freely and be in my own company, listening to outer silence as well as my inner silence. The blessing-in-disguise of the lockdowns and restrictions imposed on the world officially for health reasons presented me with many opportunities to learn about healers worldwide via a vast range of podcasts and telesummits. During this forced distancing from social life, I made the most of my time in my country home by tuning in even more deeply to spiritual realms and matters. I listened eagerly to many interviews, in which healers talked about their own life experiences, did brief readings and healings, and offered affirmations and prayers to help listeners along their paths.

During the few years since my retirement, my inner perspective of my past and myself has shifted. Instead of viewing only shame, fault, and not being good enough, I have come to the realization that my life has meaning and purpose and should be made public because many souls out there need to know about it. I have taken utmost care and asked for the Universe's assistance every time, before I started writing, to ensure the flow of my thoughts carry only memories of facts and triggered feelings. I am confident that the purpose of this writing shall be sensed for what it is meant to be—just memories revisited with compassion and forgiveness for the purpose of becoming aware of who I truly am.

My time to speak out has come, even though I still need to overcome several fears that keep me convinced that it is wiser not to publish this book, such as revealing what went on inside our home, "speaking ill" about my mother, and baring my soul. But it is human to have those fears. I sense that the time is now ripe for the whole world. After all, if I do not write about what happened to me and the way my soul responded, I would not be an example to other women, and I would fail to nudge them onto the path of forgiveness and self-awareness.

If I can let a drop fall into the pond and make ripples, no matter how small, that water shall taste different, quench thirst, and nourish the lushness of our true Mother Earth and its inhabitants.

I may not yet be able to find the gift of my life as a whole, but maybe somebody else will, for both themselves and for me. I know that I am not alone anymore and that someone out there is more than prepared to understand and resonate with what I say here. And that will be a great gift to me.

Anna Dodds
Italy, September 2023

# *Introduction*

I am aware that sharing with readers the events of my life and my memories of other lifetimes may cause pain and distress in those who, both in their knowing and unknowing, have lived similar stories of violence and abuse. Sadly, history cannot be changed. But our minds can indeed be wisely directed to change our perception of events.

In this book, I mention facts about my life that are necessary to know in order to understand how much a person can change for the better. However, for the purpose of lessening distress in readers, I have provided **trigger warnings at the beginning of chapters 3, 5, 13, 16, 17, and 27.**

Ultimately, I wish to encourage my readers to leave behind all thoughts of martyrdom and focus instead on empowerment and freedom.

Anna Dodds

# Part I: That's Life

When looking at the scraps and memorabilia that make up my past, I do not "look back." To me, the past has always been present—in my eyes, in my mind, and in the effort that I have made to carry its weight on and within my body and soul. Its weight grew as I grew up. But no matter what, my soul always refused to sigh and concede, "That's life!"

# Chapter 1

"Do you feel you have been loved?" the group leader asked.

"Yes" was the answer from each participant in the spiritual and emotional healing group; one by one, all twelve of them spoke, each delayed by one second of hesitation to find the grounding of certainty within themselves.

But I did not need one second to think. "Yes!" I answered, even though I felt that my stomach was digesting sandpaper. *Of course, I have been loved,* I thought. I misunderstood my family. It was entirely my own fault if I had not yet managed, at forty-six, to sense love within me clearly, or even the feelings that I believe make up love: the fullness of emotional nourishment, the happy memories, the alchemical consolation of a child's problem transmuted by the hug and words of an understanding adult, the strength that is learned by example....

But why on earth did I resonate so much with *Falling Leaves* by Adeline Yen Mah? Nothing like that ever happened to me! I was never mistreated or abandoned. I had lived my life in a normal, middle-class family, and I did my best to be happy about it. I didn't always manage, but my parents had always reminded me of what the whole family was sure—that I was lucky.

Not that I was lucky just by pure chance. I carried the sign of luck. My parents kept saying that I was lucky because of my big bum. Ever since I developed memory, I know I did my best to show them I was happy in a family that laughed when they said such things about me. But with time, it became harder and harder to laugh with them. Besides, my mother seemed to be absolutely obsessed with buttocks, whether mine, her own, or other people's.

However, I was the only one who noticed my mother's attitude—a fact that made me conclude that I did not have a good disposition. So I smiled even if I felt confused and hurt, and I kept my feelings to myself. After all, I did not want to show that I was difficult. Somehow, I have felt different since I was very young, but I could not understand why. I observed them, and it seemed they were all made of the same kind of dough. I lived among them. I was part of the family, but I had to try to fit in and be like them. When I was six, I even asked my mum if I was adopted. She said, "No, no," almost casually, without looking at me.

My mother was always smiling, and I smiled too. I was an obedient child, although I could not help screaming against my grandmother, who I had to obey and respect. She was Dad's mother, and there was no joking with Dad. My dad loved me, and I loved him. But when he spanked my brother, I cringed with fear and had to hold both arms on my stomach to keep demons still in my belly.

Grandmother was over seventy years old and could barely walk. She had stiff legs and shuffled her feet. In my early years before I started going to school, I accompanied her every morning to shop for food at the usual shops around the corner and across the street. I had to give her my arm to steady herself when she stepped down the pavement to cross the street. Any step, up or down, was a big effort for her.

One of the perhaps too few questions I asked my parents was: "Why does Grandma walk like that?" They told me that when she was a girl, a pan full of hot oil spilled all over her legs, which affected how she walked. I believed them, although deep down, it seemed rather odd that such an incident left consequences on her muscles and joints rather than her skin, which was smooth and had no scars. But small children believe all their good, well-meaning parents tell them.

Grandma had a croaking voice and an attitude with which I clashed. I got scared every time her booming voice suddenly called me to order. Her sudden "No!" had the power of a gunshot for a well-meaning, curious little girl like me.

But worse still was the rage that I felt toward her. She did not understand anything. She did not understand me. Her resentfulness had stiffened and shaped her upper back into a semi-spheric hunch and her mouth into a downward-pointing moon sliver. I seethed and fumed with anger toward her, even at a tender age, but I had to hold back and respect her, even if she did not meet my needs or even recognize them.

For many years, I believed that I was not sent to prep school because my brother disliked it so much that my parents had to take him out. *That's why they didn't even try with me,* I thought. But more importantly, Grandma needed company. My parents wanted me to stay at home with her to cheer her up and help her, instead of letting me be with other children at prep school.

But what was there for me to do at home, on the seventh floor of a block of flats, while my brother was at school and my parents were at work? There was a girl on the same floor that I considered as a friend. We talked to each other, as we stood on our flats' kitchen balconies on opposite sides of the inner courtyard of the block, across the hanging wash and pots of geraniums. It was fun to chat with her and her older sister.

One day her sister rang our doorbell, and I opened the door for her. Perhaps I knew that it would be her at the door, as I was not allowed to open the door at the tender age of four. She took my hand, and I followed her. I followed my heart. It was so good to be with my two little friends at their home and to play with them. They were one and two years older than me and led the games.

Then I was called home. My grandmother and mother were standing in the entrance hall. My grandma's mouth was pointing even more downward. Mother had just returned from work, or perhaps she had been told to go home at once. She said something to minimize what was happening, but the pressure I was sensing from them was too much for me to bear, and I burst into bawling sobs. I perceived the message that I had done something wrong. It was wrong that I had followed my heart.

My mother's way of minimizing things always turned a knife of guilt and shame in my belly. It was a technique to command the feelings of a little child to disappear and make no more noise and bother adults no more. But having my feelings pushed under the carpet made me very wary of making mistakes. In my subconscious, mistakes were never just inevitable learning devices along the uncharted path of life. They were heavy burdens that I should have known better to avoid altogether.

So, what could I do on my own locked in at home? For sure, I was happy and privileged to live on the top floor of that block of flats. We had a view of the hills surrounding Genoa to the north—each one with a fortress on top, the elegant Liberty blocks of flats on the hillside to the east, and our street below with large flowerbeds dividing the lanes all the way to the seafront to the south. But I wanted the company of someone who could play and chat and laugh with me.

One day I had an idea: I would talk to myself. This became an addiction that did not leave me for the rest of my life. It was great! It was like having just the right friend to talk to about the things that I wanted to tell at that moment while playing exactly the game that I wanted. I moved around and danced, all the while whispering and laughing to myself.

I had time to spare, and I used it to contemplate the blue sky, the swallows, the clouds, the hills, the skyline, and the sea. And I listened to silence.

Music made me happy. The part of the day I enjoyed most with my grandmother was when the radio transmissions started in the afternoon. We listened to music together. I learned jingles by heart, and when I sang them, the adults in the family would laugh. I never understood why they laughed. After all, it was my grandmother who told me to sing, and I did. Why would they laugh? What had I done? I had just done what they asked me to do.

Playing with my brother was what I sought instinctively. However, I always ended up crying. Every single time we began playing together, I eagerly went along with what he suggested, which, more often than not, ended up with me not just losing but also being laughed at. Seven years my elder, he was smarter than me. He learned things at school and from his schoolmates that were not what my heart needed. I was naive and always fell for his jokes and pranks, such as ending up with my hands smeared with glue. I have

# PART I: THAT'S LIFE

always hated having sticky hands! Losing every time made me feel like I just didn't get it and I never would. He may have been the bully, but I was the unbearably annoying one.

I loved Dad. He got up early in the morning, just like me. And on Sundays, he would take the whole family on a trip to the hills and the countryside to play. He smoked the whole time while driving there. When it was time to go back home, I often felt sick and vomited. My mother always blamed that on something I shouldn't have eaten—something different from what I usually ate. But at the end of a fun day, I could sense the change in the energy from the morning, and I felt it even more when I entered our home.

It felt like there was an invisible screen at the entrance door that stole all the good energy I carried within myself. The energy at home had to be of a certain kind. No show of uncontrolled happiness was allowed except from small children. When I was growing up, they made sure that I grew up correctly.

"Laughter abounds on fools' lips," my grandma said.

"It is not good that you are so happy about a new dress. That is being shallow," my mother said.

"Do not pull faces," my father said with an expression of outright dislike.

My brother had more fun than me playing with his schoolmate, who happened to live in the same block and regularly visited every afternoon.

The atmosphere at home was heavy for a good reason. My late uncle was mentioned often, and so was Grandfather. There were mementos of both my uncle and grandfather that were kept as cherished heirlooms. There were my uncle's wooden construction blocks and fishing rods. Grandfather's office furniture was now my brother's bedroom furniture, while I inherited my brother's desk and chair.

My uncle was my father's little brother. He fought in World War II and never came back. I did not understand the extent of the sorrow for the loss of a dear one, nor did I know what it meant to go through years of war. The hunger, the bombardments, the destruction, the death toll, and what it was like to be a prisoner of war were the memories that my elders often would recall as a comparison to the present times. I was made aware that Italy was being reborn. There was food, and there was money—though both were to be used sparingly. We were finally free to live safely. However, in the early 1960s, when I was five to ten years old, I could distinctly feel that a lingering undertone of war and life under a dictatorship remained. There was still a distinction between superiority and inferiority and stigma for religious and political reasons. Consequently, repressed feelings and a sense of duty still permeated the air and controlled actions, as well as the way people thought and behaved.

Grandma was stiffened in sorrow. She never had a gesture or words of affection for anyone. She was the daughter of an aristocrat, and in my childish mind, I supposed that was the way upper-class people behaved.

*Seriously? Look at her!* She was as dowdy as could be, with holes in her brown-gray dress that she never mended. Her voice and manners betrayed her total ignorance of both kindness and language. She spoke, translating clumsily from her Sicilian dialect, and used loudness to provoke obedience, especially from me. My rage toward her was too big for my age.

Yes, I know; I had to obey others because I was a child. I had to learn to restrict myself and not scream so loudly and get so angry, but I did. However, one thing I noticed when I did that was that I was much more powerful than they were. I was no match for them. The power of my feelings, the power of my reactions, the fury of my anger, were greater than me and greater than them. I dimmed my power to fit in.

I felt too much pressure to behave differently from the ways I instinctively did, which made me cry so much that I thought there must be something wrong about living. It was not right that a child my age cried that much.

From my early childhood, I fantasized about escaping from home. I could see myself, dressed in the pretty smock my mother sewed for me, safely walking alone up the avenue into the city, without being noticed. But I knew it was just a dream and that I must never do that, lest their attitude toward me become sterner.

One afternoon, my parents took me with them to visit one of Dad's colleagues in his home. All my life, I have remembered the atmosphere of fullness that I breathed at their place. The light was different, and the air was full of an energy that made my heart expand. My heart had room to breathe, and I took in that sweetness, as that was what my soul needed. There was greenery in the neighborhood, a whole side of a hill with houses and their gardens. In a corner of the sitting room, I remember a small table covered by a tasteful tablecloth with colorful flowers and leaves all the way down to the floor. The care for that corner in the apartment has sat in my heart ever since as a symbol of love, creativity, and an expression of happiness.

I was four years of age when I visited that home, and when it was time to leave, I told my parents, "I am staying here." They laughed, of course. What else could they do at my unexpected demand? Dad's colleague and his wife insisted that my parents come and pick me up later. They loved children. They so wanted children of their own, but they had not been blessed.

So I could stay a bit longer in that atmosphere that nourished and sustained me. I just toddled about the house, taking in the energies of the place. The lady of the house was of a fuller size than the women in my home. When we happened to cross paths, her heart expanded and opened a smile on her lips, and widened her eyes subtly to take in more of the marvelous surprise of seeing a child before her.

How nourishing is a glimpse of the infinite, even for a brief terrestrial second.

\* \* \*

My father always said that I was "strong-headed." He said that lovingly, like a nickname for me. However, there was a "but." Repetition of the same words over time conveyed to me the energy of those words that meant it would be more appropriate and acceptable if I said yes to what elders proposed for me. If I said "no," it meant that I was being annoying. Even worse, if I didn't like things, then I was being difficult.

I did not like the way my brother behaved with them as he grew up. He was defiant and demanding, with an attitude of righteous and angry silence. I could never be like him. I would never behave like that with my parents.

Mother always turned to me, saying, "You are my joy!" with a loving smile and tone of voice.

My father called me Annuccia—little cute Anna. What a pretty nickname for a little girl. Another nickname that was used quite often for me was Nannazza. The sound is completely different, as is its energy. It is an application of the suffix *-azza,* meaning too big to be pretty or of normal size, to a vernacular form of my name. My father's side of the family spoke the Sicilian dialect that uses the term *bambinazza* to mean a "big, fat little girl."

Hearing Nannazza did not seem strange to me when I was small. But as time passed, I realized that it was not a *name* I was called by. It was a *term* pronounced with the energy and intention that its suffix expressed, even if always sugarcoated by smiles and giggles.

The nickname they used for my brother was Bambo, a short form of *bambino,* that is, male child.

I always had a good appetite. I enjoyed everything that was put on the table and in my dish. Unlike children who eat like birds or refuse food, I was never a problem for my parents. It seemed to me that my mother was unsure about my request to eat more, while my grandmother did not seem to have any qualms about saying no to my requests. My brother, instead, was difficult and would not eat fruit or vegetables. One day, Grandmother peeled an orange for him and left it on the kitchen table as a treat that would entice him. One by one, the slivers began to disappear from the plate. "Sshh!" whispered Grandmother to my mother. "He is eating it!"

"No," I said. "I am!"

They sort of laughed, but somehow I learned there and then that I must not touch the food that was prepared especially for him.

# Chapter 2

Dad was driving. We were all proud of owning a car at the end of the 1950s. We did not need to take trains anymore.

There was an air so different from home. I felt very small among adults who were a bit lost in an environment that was new to them too. I just followed along. I was sensing and perceiving my surroundings differently than before. For a change, memories stayed in my mind, and views and voices were being impressed like movies in my…in my what? Memory? Soul?

I was growing…I was already three years old. That's what growing is: feeling that I had changed, looking back, and realizing that I saw other people's attitudes differently through lenses that I did not wear but did have somewhere within me. I was no longer reacting. I had accumulated information about the forces that exist between adults. I was wary at times of some subtle hues of behavior that whispered to me, "Be careful." There were always so many adults around me. They were everywhere, and they were always the majority. I was smaller and alone. They thought differently. They did not sense what I sensed. But how could they not? A need is a need. It is the most important and strongest drive at any given moment. I needed to feel safer, calmer. Instead, they gave me the impression that they cared for their own needs but did so with an unsure and hesitant inner energy that told me they needed guidance too. I was following untrained guides.

They just went on doing their best.

I did not know how far we were from home—maybe many hours,

many kilometers. I did not know why we were there at that beautiful spot. It seemed that those surroundings must be the destination of our journey. I have no memory of what went on between home and there. Perhaps I slept all the way and woke up where Christmas trees grow.

We went into a wooden house. I was given a glass bottle of soda and a straw. I liked that drink. It was made of fruit. I played with the straw in the bottle that had just been popped open, and foam overflowed and spilled all over the wooden floor. There was no reaction from the adults, both my parents and their friends. Not a word was said in between the spilling and my bursting into a loud bawl.

How did I know that I shouldn't have done that? Why did my feelings explode into a flashing red alert? What had accumulated inside of me to trigger a gush of unbearable pressure?

Nothing happened even after I started crying. I am pretty sure that I was not scolded or criticized for acting like a three-year-old. But perhaps in one little corner of my soul, there is a tiny slip of paper that still embodies my mother's embarrassment over my behavior.

\* \* \*

Every summer, we went on holiday in the hills and stayed at hotels. There I would find children to play with. It was okay for me to play with one little friend at a time, but not in a company larger than three. As I grew, I noticed that I did not like children. In fact, sometimes I could not stand them, although I was a child myself. I needed to be with my parents all the time to feel that I was an immovable part of them.

While we were voyaging on the ship to Southern Italy, I would have felt excluded and discarded if my parents had sent me to play at the nursery with other children under the supervision of a female childminder wearing a white coat like a doctor. I was seven, and I would have felt deeply offended if they had put me at a little lunch table with other children instead of seating me at the lunch table with them and other adults. I would have felt less-than, different, and not worthy of being considered one in the circle of the adults. Deep down, I would have felt rejected.

Throughout my life, my mother would repeat a remark that my grandmother said with wry laughter when children became too much to bear: "Children…aren't they lovely?"

\* \* \*

After my mother had my brother, her mother encouraged her, "Have a little girl," and when finally my mother got pregnant again, everybody in the family was deeply worried that she would produce a boy again. No one was allowed to compete with my brother, who was to be the one and only son, the living proof of the return of Dad's little brother. Dad's mother brought home the news that some neighbors had just had a daughter after their son, and she cuttingly remarked, "They sure can do things the right way!" I had to be female. If I had been a boy, I heard—not just once—that I would have been treated spitefully.

From a very early age, I insisted that I wanted to wear shorts instead of dresses, and I was not interested in playing with dolls. My Southern Mediterranean features included dark brown hair, but I shouted back, "I am blonde!" to whomever complimented me as a pretty brunette.

My mother's way of showing her affection to me never changed throughout her life. She would twist and protrude her jaw to one side, look at me intently and sternly, and distort her words as if she was talking like a child. Then she would say, "Pretty, her. A bit daft." She made me laugh every time until I entered a stage of my adulthood when I realized there was something unwholesome in those words. Besides, distorting words was her peculiarity throughout her life.

She was careful about complimenting me. She was a primary school teacher and had studied pedagogy, so she knew what was needed to educate children well. Sometimes, when I was still a toddler, she would tell me, "I say to you that you are cute because I am your mum, but you do know that you are unattractive, don't you?" I would assent, "Yes, yes, of course." Perhaps that was her method for making sure that I did not become vain.

Her small range of loving expressions also included "cute big face," which she would exclaim to me with a tone of amazement and wide-open hands, all the way into my forties.

I was happy when my mother expressed her love for me. Many times I would talk to her about things that were important to me. After maybe half a minute of holding her attention, I would see her face change and turn assertive with aggressive eyes. At the same time, she protruded her jaw, shifted it to one side, and softly scraped my lower cheek with her nail tips until she bunched her fingers and stated, "So cute!"—of course, while distorting the words in a childish tone of voice. That was the death of what I was saying to her and the end of her listening to me. At other times, she would "correct" my facial expression while disregarding what I was saying to her.

* * *

My mother often visited nice shops to buy me clothes that were pretty, tasteful, and good quality. But I also wore my brother's sweaters that he had outgrown and hand-me-downs from my cousins that my maternal grandmother had deemed were still good to wear.

She laughed at the size of the panties she had to buy for me. She said she needed to buy me a size that was for a child many years older than me. I did not share her laughter; in fact, it made me anxious. She shut her eyes tight, averted her face, and sometimes bit her tongue to repress laughter, uttering no sounds. That made me think my size was so exaggerated that just a ha-ha laugh was not enough. She had to hold back, or she would have rolled on the floor and laughed herself to tears. There was a ticklish element underlying her way of laughing about that particular aspect of my existence, as if she had a one-track mind about it.

I felt so good the day that she bought me a pair of emerald-green linen trousers. I put them on as soon as we got home. When Dad arrived from work, I greeted him at the entrance as usual but kept a certain distance to show him the new buy. My mother was there beside him and told me, "Let's have a turnaround...." I did but turned toward them again when I heard Dad giggling and exclaiming, "Gosh!" Then I saw my mother's face and how self-satisfied she was. She kept her lips closed and twisted in a held-back smile as she looked down on me.

I would laugh and play with my mother, sing and dance with her, and go on walks and learn the names of plants from her. And she would kiss me with the loudest possible smack she could, on the opposite side of her lips so as not to smear my cheek with her red lipstick. But when it was a matter of obeying her and having to accept what she told me, I felt so stripped of all happiness that I would think, *She treats me as if I have no soul.* Perhaps if I were stronger or had a sweeter disposition, I would not have felt so unhappy with such a good—or should I say perfect—mother.

During my childhood and youth, I felt very distinctly that I had a weight on my heart. In my mind, I saw it like a heavy stone wedge pointing down to keep my heart sunken. When I was nervous and anxious, I could feel my heart racing just above my belly button. I never knew what it meant to have my heart in my mouth.

Indeed, as I grew, my inability grew to continue laughing with my mother about my shape, behavior, posture, mood, habits, ways, and facial expressions—in two words, my existence. It especially took me aback when she made other people laugh at me in my presence.

I felt so stupid in those moments. I never saw it coming, no matter how many times it happened, again and again. I could not help being what I was, and she would find that a laughing matter. She was my mother, and I knew she was a good mother and better than other mothers. Then why did I feel hurt and incapable of laughing with them? If they laughed, I thought, they meant well. They did no harm. They were just having a moment of hilarity, which was always started by my ever-smiling mother. The problem with stupidity is that there is no cure for it. It is impossible to wake up intelligent one day. I found it next to impossible to not hate myself for being born stupid.

I did not hate myself for being born that shape, though. I simply did not know what to do about it. I envisioned a machine that would make bodies perfect. It consisted of two halves of a human body, front and back, in which a child could be clamped for a few minutes. Then they would exit with a perfectly shaped body and the proportions of the standard beauty of the time. But that was in my imagination; it did not exist in reality anywhere in the world.

My mother was the one who kept the family happy. She laughed and said things that made everybody laugh, especially when she distorted words. She told me that she even laughed in her dreams. Sometimes she was so good at acting that I mistook her joking for something serious. Like when we reached home, she would look for the key in her handbag. She could never find the key first thing. She would stick her hand in her handbag and exclaim, "Oh, my God, the keys!" as if she had been pickpocketed in a moment of distraction over the several hours that we had been out. What frightened me was her standing taller than me, slightly bent over me, and grimacing with one eye almost closed and the other eye open and staring at me.

I fell for it every time. Every single time, I felt my body chemistry change for the worse. Yet she was just imitating her own mother as she remembered her mother's peculiar antics. I was so dismayed at my innate inability to detect that she was faking. And I did not see why I always felt physically changed for the worse, while anybody else would have just waited and then smiled at her finding the key or would have rolled their eyes and said, "Here we go again."

She fooled me every time because she had a natural talent for impersonation. She consistently reported what other people had said to her by imitating their accent, voice, mouth movements, facial expressions, and the way they held themselves. Uncle was very good at that too. Obviously, they played at that when they were children and could not stop as adults. They made the whole family laugh heartily at their caricaturing the people they knew.

However, as I grew and experienced life, I saw that "happy" attitude differently. First, such a habit should only be shown in private. But when a habit is formed, it is difficult not to behave automatically in that way in public too. Consequently, I had to be very mindful and stop for a moment before reporting what somebody else had said to me. Speaking clearly was more important than taking center stage and making others laugh.

## PART I: THAT'S LIFE

I became aware of the importance of behaving in private the same way as I would behave in public. As I stopped imitating other people's peculiarities, I noticed that I had been judgmental of them and mocked them. Mocking means that I cannot stand what somebody else does. *That is disrespectful*, I thought. It is important to grow up and behave properly at home so as to be comfortable in public too.

Impersonation has its proper place on stage. My mother would have been successful if she had turned her talent into a career. But considering the performing arts as a career was outlandish in my family. Being visible attracts envy, and by performing, you go hungry.

A subtle suspicion began hissing inside of me. *What if my mother is childish? What if she mocks others because she dislikes them? And worst of all, what if she impersonates me?*

I made sure that I was absolutely perfect and irreprehensible in my behavior. I took in all that other parents told her about their children behaving laudably and then did it to the best of my ability. My mother reported such news with an intensity of expression, which I took as the parents' true words and feelings. For example, an elder sister, with a slight intellectual disability, was seen choosing the best cherries to give her little—preferred—sister. I began eating only the broken biscuits and leaving the whole ones for my brother, hoping that somebody would notice. Nobody did. A cousin was consistently performing at school beyond expectations. Ah, that was a tough one for me to follow.

By the way, I did not ever hear my mother speaking about her children on the phone. From my bedroom, which was just a few steps from the telephone, I could listen to the telephone conversations that my mother had with other mothers. Hearing my mother change the subject made me sorrowful, even if I knew very well that she was considerate of others and would ask them questions, as is elegant to do in polite society. She would not talk about herself or her family matters.

\* \* \*

I was creative even at a young age. I grew up watching my mother machine-sewing dresses for herself and me, which she had learned from her mother. I loved to create things with my own hands out of paper and fabric, and to read books and magazines that gave instructions on how to make toys. I made stuffed animals using felt, including a red seahorse my father carried in his wallet for good luck all his life. I learned to knit and embroider. With time, I became very good at crocheting. But as I grew up, my father hated that I kept busy that way. The only expression of creativity my father would have liked me to take up was painting.

There was a bit of talk going on in the family about increasing my interest in that form of art. Then one day, my mother took me to a specialized shop where we chose a fine wooden case with lots of oil colors, brushes, and a palette. We also bought a book to learn how to paint horses. But it all ended in nothing within a couple of years. I did not have an inner drive for painting. I was just given tools in my hands and did not know what to do with them. Besides, being a very tidy person, I could not conceive of mixing colors and making a mess with them.

Dad also insisted that I should learn how to swim. I was not exactly enthusiastic at the prospect, but my mother agreed with him and took me to the only place where swimming lessons were available during the school year: the pools of the National Olympic Committee.

My previous swimming experience had consisted of going to the beach with my mother every summer. I always used an inflatable donut to dip my feet in the ever-wavy sea, into which my mother never accompanied me. And now, at eight years of age, I had to undergo a medical for competitive swimming, which included running, falling to the ground and getting up, and breathing into a tube.

The swimming hall reeked with chlorine and loudly echoed with the shouting of the instructors. The accompanying mums were watching on the steps way above the pool, which looked like a long and narrow well.

My mother had wondered if the instructor assigned to my group of girls was an Olympian. Whatever her level of swimming, her personality was almost identical to my grandmother's. She shouted instructions to us while standing on the edge of the pool. I was frazzled by the echoing noise, the shouting, the depth and temperature of the water, the splashing of the other girls which caused waves and sprays, and the levels of bleach that reeked and turned the water yellow and irritated my eyes.

The other girls had no problems at all and followed every instruction they were given, while I was so full of fear. I could hear my mother complimenting the mother of my classmate: "Oooh, what a fish!" By the third lesson, I used a weapon that I had never used before and would never use again—I cried. Yes, I cried to be left alone. The instructor was spiteful, both in words and behavior, but did leave me alone.

My mother dried and changed me in the locker room, which was full of the noise of chatting and hot air blasting out from hair dryers. Not one word was exchanged while she drove me home. She did not take me to swimming lessons there again, nor did I hear one word about it from her or Dad.

The summer came, and the idea of swimming lessons reemerged. My mother took me to the ever-reeking, open-air pools of the Olympic Committee, where I found a much nicer teacher. I changed into my swimming costume and got ready to enter the water. I turned to my side and saw my mother talking to the swimming instructor; both were looking and laughing at me from a distance. She told the instructor that she could not help but laugh at the size of my bum, which was so big that it kept my costume away from my back.

I heard her laugh about this subject many times over the years. She was always standing next to another person and at a distance from me, looking down on me sideways.

# Chapter 3

**Trigger Warning:
This chapter contains descriptions of sexual violence, which some readers may find distressing.**

School was one activity that was mentioned all the time. No surprise—my mother was a primary school teacher, and my brother was already attending school. My own time for going to school inevitably arrived. I am not sure I was happy about the idea of going to school. More likely, it was a perspective that was mentioned by adults as something exciting for me. It was a sign that I was growing up, and therefore, my life needed to change. I just went along like a sheep following its shepherd. We all heard the shepherd dog barking in our souls, "You must go to school!"

The school was an old building near home, up the avenue with tall sycamore trees on both sides. The building had been specially constructed at the beginning of the last century to house public offices. On one side, there was the Vital Statistics Office, while at the back, overlooking a square, was the entrance to the primary school. It was an austere building, built to be functional and no fun. There were lots of classrooms and large hallways with high ceilings. There was no gym in those days. But the fun happened outside, on the square, where we could run and play under the refreshing canopy of the sycamore trees that guarded us from the then light traffic.

The children walked up the steps to the third floor, where the classrooms were, and many stopped at the window on the first floor to wave good-bye to their parents. The few times that my dad took me to that school, he always insisted that I stop at that window and wave at him. Then he would go to work.

My first day was not the easiest. I recall that my mother, who was always late all her life, took me to my first day of school when school had already begun a week before. Not only that, we arrived there when the bell had already rung. She accompanied me to the classroom, where I saw twenty-five six-year-old girls in their white cotton uniforms staring at me from their desks. The teacher, who knew my mother well because they were colleagues, introduced me, and I had to sit down and adjust. She was an unmarried woman approaching retirement age; I liked her almost immediately. She was Jewish, and I was the only child in the class to know what had to be kept secret. I never said a word to my classmates, as I knew how important it was not to disclose that particular detail of hers—not even sixteen years after the end of World War II and of the fascist regime.

I liked my schoolmates too. But by second grade, I did not want to go to school any longer. When I said so to my parents, they couldn't help but laugh.

Back then, it was compulsory to wear a uniform. For the teachers, it was a black cotton coat. For us girls, it was a smock made of white cotton, with buttons and a gracefully knotted belt at the back. That would prevent us from staining our clothes and wearing them out. However, the underlying truth was to equalize and standardize us all, besides concealing the differences in status and wealth that our clothes would have clearly shown.

But it is inevitable to make comparisons. At school, differences are inevitably made between who is "good" and who is "slow," and between those who are good at something and those who are not. I was good at almost everything, thank God. I could already read and write. I had learned lots of notions while I was at home, entertaining myself, and my brother would tell me about what he was learning at his school.

However, I never had the courage to stand in front of the class and recite the homework to the teacher. I could not bear to see the whole class staring at me and maybe have the teacher correct my mistakes. Not knowing something, or realizing that I failed to come up with the right answer, left me full of shame, insecurity, and anxiety. That is how I always felt when we had to write a composition, since first grade. My anxiety grew more and more every time a composition was on the agenda.

I was never a chatty child. Besides, what could I have learned from my grandmother? Talking with her was no preparatory exercise to organize thoughts and write well. I just could not fill the pages with ink. I felt sick when some schoolmates said that they wanted to be journalists when they grew up. Asking questions and writing was so alien to me. I never asked questions; I never questioned what I was told to do. I believed authority figures, and even when I sensed that what they said made me smaller and restricted, I knew it was safer to go along with their will.

My teacher told my mother that I was shallow. I did not ask why, as I knew well what shallow meant. It meant being happy with material things. I loved the things that I had. I was simply happy for the things that I had, and I preferred to dedicate myself to what I liked rather than to what made me insecure. I sensed my teacher's quick labeling as an inability to read beyond the behavior of a child. But I also sensed her jealousy at what we—the new generation born after WWII—had, which was more than what her generation had. We had more things to play with, the freedom to ask for something, and the luck to obtain it.

So, if showing happiness equals shallowness, I chose to be cautious at what I said. I hid my feelings, and behaved more like they did. I had to show that I was intelligent at all costs. Not only that, I also had to be smart. That meant that I must not talk about what I had or what we had at home, nor about what we were likely to do in the near future. Dad instructed me to just say, "I don't know." Denying and hiding were smart moves. Later in life, I would understand that his attitude was all about self-defense.

* * *

My mother went to work only in the morning. We could be together the rest of the day. The fun side of being with my mother in the afternoon was going out together. Sometimes she took me to the park. Sometimes she took me to visit her mother and uncle's family at their flat. It was a drive or a long ride on the bus. They lived in one of the prettiest neighborhoods of the city, in the flat where my mother and her brother grew up.

My maternal grandmother was very loving. She smiled with genuine joy at all her grandchildren. But she was also strict and had a natural propensity to irritability and being commanding that made her endearing to all of us, though maybe Mother and Uncle felt more like rolling their eyes.

I could play and chat for hours with my cousins, two girls who were a few years older than me. Then one day, a third girl arrived. For me, she arrived out of the blue. I had been told absolutely nothing that another little cousin was on her way, nor had I seen my aunt for many months.

Other than my cousins, I had a little girlfriend my age who was the daughter of a colleague of my dad's. I often visited her at her flat, and we had great fun playing. I even stayed on for dinner once without my parents. We also went on holiday together to the mountains. Her dad even had a camera and took photos of us.

I heard the grown-ups say that her mother was older than my mother and that she and her husband had to wait many years before their daughter was born. That did not make sense to me, but I do not ever remember asking for clarification.

Back in those days, being younger than another woman was regarded as something to be proud of. It was not uncommon that "older" women would take a couple of years from their age. Never ask a lady how old she is; that is rude. That was the excuse to never talk about becoming less desirable. That is how a woman growing old was regarded. Becoming wiser with age was completely overlooked. What mattered was only youth, good looks, and a pleasing disposition. In fact, being a bit daft was all right and maybe even preferable.

I did, therefore, not regard it as a coincidence that the few ladies whom my mother called "very intelligent" turned out to be so unattractive that they had failed to find husbands or, rather, that no bachelors would choose them as their wives. One of these ladies was the pediatrician that my mother chose for me. My mother spoke highly of that doctor, adding that she loved me so much. She came across as a professional who was self-confident in her competence and had poised manners. Instead, I sensed an unfeeling nature with a tad of revenge.

She may have been in her early forties, but if I compare her to women nowadays, she could look in her early seventies if it were not for her brown hair. She was a diminutive figure, thin and hunching. She wore thick eyeglasses with brown-tinted lenses that enabled her to see only from a very short distance. I never recall her eyes looking at my mother while talking to her. I do not remember her touching me either because of the freezing fear that I kept harnessed in those moments. My fear took on the appearance of a sheepish, good girl while a thought at the back of my head attempted to convince me that everything would be okay and that the doctor would find nothing wrong with me. I knew I had to comfort myself because my mother would say, "Don't be silly! You are being silly," without looking at me, in a tone of superiority.

What was beyond me was that my mother had to ask someone else if her daughter was ill or well—someone who saw me once every few months, while my mother had me under her eyes all the time. Once she took me there because I was dotted all over with red spots. The doctor eyed me as best she could and diagnosed me with a rash caused by strawberries. I was forbidden to touch the strawberries regularly placed on the dining table. I was scolded when I was caught pinching one from the bowl. A few days later, my father noticed lots of mosquitoes in my room and eventually realized that my rash was not caused by strawberries, but rather I was being sucked dry by mosquitoes. I was free to eat strawberries again.

Another time, my mother noticed little bubbles full of liquid on my fingers and was angrily embarrassed that I looked like "a mangy dog." She took me to that doctor, who said nothing, as she had never seen sun rash before, maybe not even in the medical books of her time.

More importantly, when I was one year old, my mother noticed I was not teething, so she took me to that doctor. All her life, she would repeat to me every so often that I had good teeth because that doctor ordered a course of injections to help them grow.

In my early childhood, my mother gave injections to everybody in the family, including herself, every day. Seeing the syringe boiling in the kitchen in the morning was as normal as making coffee. It was no problem giving injections to my brother, who considered it one of the daily things to do in life, such as washing, eating, or drinking. But with me, she had to use special tactics. I did not have daily injections, as she would have liked, but she would surprise me by perhaps inviting her mother over, or by taking me to see her doctor brother, and then holding me for the real purpose of the visit. She had to resort to such tactics because I was not as good as my brother was. "When he was your age, he had boxes and boxes of injections!"

Whenever she talked to acquaintances about my silly fear, she never failed to add that I liked being injected in my butt sooo much when I was a baby and claimed that she did not know why or when I became fearful.

While looking at old photos, we found one with me as a baby sitting on her lap. She commented that it was taken at the time when I had the injections for my teeth. That's what a photo of herself with her baby daughter inspired her to recall.

She missed an opportunity when I contracted typhoid at the age of seven. She called in a doctor who did house calls who prescribed injections and that we clear all toys from my room because he saw too much dust. Those injections were special, which meant that my mother could not give them herself but had to call in a specialist. That woman seemed to be a cleaning lady who loved to chat with my parents. I wrestled every time to the best of my ability, but two adults against one child always win with physical strength and, above all, manipulative lies.

None of the adults in my family had thought of dusting or maybe even cleaning one of my dear stuffed animals to override the doctor's orders and make me feel the comfort of a hug. I was grown, and that meant that I could do without toys if told to, as well as stop asking my mother to pick me up and hug me. I was heavy and should not be clingy.

# PART I: THAT'S LIFE

\* \* \*

Visiting the doctor or the dentist was as normal as visiting family. My mother took my brother and me to the dentist every week. Later in life, both my mother and my brother realized that our dentist was not only no good but also dishonest for insisting that we visit him every week so that he could earn more money. My father heard comments and even a nickname about him at that time and told my mother, but it just all ended in sniggering at gossip.

My mother had a fine denture. She had taken seriously the advice she had received from other women in her family, back when she was a girl, that she should always be smiling.

She wrapped each milk tooth of mine that fell out in a tiny piece of paper, wrote the date on it, and kept them all in a small jewelry box. After all, they were the precious product of injections, not of nature.

I was elated when I saw the coins that the tooth fairy left for me. But the teeth that grew as a replacement for my milk teeth were not satisfactory. I thought that there was nothing wrong with them. I could chew fine, and I smiled as instructed by my mother, especially when photos were taken of me. But I kept hearing the adults in the family talking about my teeth, and I developed the feeling that something about me needed improvement. So one day, my mother took me to the dentist to have my teeth straightened.

I may have been nine when I started wearing braces. This was not without pain or side effects. Unfortunately, no adult, whether the dentist himself or the adults in my family, including my grandmother who wore a denture, gave me guidance on how to care for the braces so that it would be sanitary to put them in my mouth all night long. I just bit them, and I had to continue wearing the braces even if they rubbed against mouth sores.

I never had guidance on how to take care of my teeth as a small child. It was only when I was four or five years of age that I was told that I should brush my teeth every day. I do not recall brushing my teeth before at all. Maybe Mum did it for me, but I really do not remember a toothbrush in my mouth being maneuvered by an adult. I do remember how she washed my face, though, and how I gasped for air while she hurriedly rubbed her soapy hand up and down with little regard for the protrusion of my nose or my breath, and then rubbed again with wet hands to rinse.

Ever since I began to brush my teeth, I have never changed how I feel about toothpaste. I still cannot stand the texture or the taste of toothpaste, and I cannot conceive for the life of me how it is possible that people rush to brush their teeth after their meals to replace the taste of food with the taste of chemicals.

Wearing an orthodontic appliance for straightening teeth is not a matter of a few months. I had to wear it for years. It was a gentle, and sometimes not so gentle, continuous battle against nature. What grows naturally in a certain position and follows a certain direction tends to return to its original position and direction, as programmed by the person's DNA. I had subtle emotional side effects from wearing that thing in my mouth over an extended period. First of all, I was defective. Improvement was necessary. It was a tool for me to bite and shut up. It was one of society's invasive methods to shape a child into being acceptable.

Several years went on, and my mother, as the wise house accountant that she was, kept a record of all the expenses required for straightening my teeth, as best they could allow. For many, many years, she would tell me how much she loved my straightened teeth. As was her way of showing her love and affection to me, she would put on a facial expression of serious assertiveness. Then she would distort the words "pretty little teeth" like a child would, and, bunching her fingers on my teeth, she would swiftly move them to her mouth as if to kiss them. Invariably, she dropped the barb, "The 300,000 lira teeth!"

I guess that today that would amount to about half a year's average primary teacher's salary. Today any dentist would first estimate the total expenditure, and indeed any parent would request it and assess it before committing. But it was not so back in those days. So, in a sense, I was responsible for costing my mother so much money, more than she ever expected and was prepared to fork out. And money was important, more important than feelings.

All the while, our diet was composed of the simple natural food that Grandmother cooked for us, plus the sweet treats that Mother made sure were ever-present at home or available as a snack when going out. Candies were staple nibbles at our home. Sugar in hot drinks was abundant. My brother and I grew up consuming a quantity of sugar that caused cavities in our teeth since we were children, hence our regular visits to the dentist.

It was only my mother who had been brought up on sweets. My father was brought up eating bread and steaks and did not care for sweet foods all through his life. I do not recall Grandmother ever baking.

\* \* \*

There was a side to my mother that frightened me. But not because she frightened me, oh no. That would never be the case. It was me who responded in that way regarding what was right to do and what was a good mother's right to do to her own child.

A good mother would wash her daughter, and so my mother washed me. She gave me a bath once a week, being overcareful that I would not get cold, rubbing the towel all over my skin, and sometimes telling me to put myself in bed under the blankets in order to warm up again. I guess she did not want me to get pneumonia, which her father had died from.

She also washed my private parts after I went to the bathroom, that is, after I had my daily poo. She would turn on the hot water tap of the bidet and wash me with soap with one finger, making sure that the pressure and rubbing of her finger alone would clean me perfectly.

The water would run warmer and hotter, and the pressure of her finger would have me react and try to close my legs in an attempt to protect my soft private parts. She would then run a bit of cold water to lower the temperature, but that middle finger and her attitude had more rights than I had. Once, I just told her that I did not want to be washed. She became angry and threatened to tell everybody I was a dirty girl. She said so in her usual way of scolding me by whispering her reproach. It was bad enough to be scolded for something so bad that neighbors must not hear, but the prospect of everybody knowing that I was dirty was worse still and, in fact, unbearable.

She was extremely attentive to hygiene and rather squeamish, especially with her facial expressions and voice. She was very careful to ensure that I never stepped on spit or dung.

When we went out and about together, we would stay out for hours. I was little and needed to go for a wee at some point. So she would find a toilet, and she would place strips of toilet paper for me to sit safely and cleanly on, where who knows who had sat before. She would stay there with me, and when I finished my business, she would not use fresh, clean toilet paper to wipe me dry. Instead, she would fold that same paper that was on the seat and use it to clean me dry, thus passing the message to me that my private parts were as disgusting and unsanitary as a public toilet.

One day, while I was sitting on the toilet, I was looking at my groin. It occurred to me that I had never touched it, so I did with one hand. I touched myself very gently, with the hand of a four-year-old, but I instinctively reacted by bending over to protect my lower abdomen against my thighs, from the ticklish sensation of invasive, unwanted touch that felt so odd. I touched myself carefully all over my lower abdomen, and I had the same reaction over and over. I did not touch myself again, not even to ease that tension.

Touching myself with my hands became out of the question. I became squeamish about my own private parts. When I learned to wash myself, I did it with a sponge.

Children may behave instinctively in ways that may be embarrassing for adults. My embarrassing behavior consisted of touching my crotch with my hand, as if I needed to comfort it in a moment of shyness in the presence of an adult who was talking to me. I would move my hand in front of my skirt and then press it against my crotch, thus feeling some protection. The last time I did that was in front of my mother's headmaster. She asked me to stop doing that with an embarrassed, grimacing smile that was meant to be a gentle, educating no-no to a six-year-old.

# Chapter 4

Toy shops were magic worlds where imagination could be unleashed. Just by looking at the shop window, my heart expanded with the colors, the variety, and the abundance of what was contained in that space.

But buying toys was a different matter. I remember how fearful I would be when my father answered my requests with, "I have no money." I did not understand he meant, "No, I won't buy you that." I thought that this was a genuine piece of information he was giving me about the current financial situation of the family, and I became afraid that we wouldn't have enough food to eat or be able to have any fun.

Asking my mother was different. We would go out together and not only dream in front of the shop windows but also go inside sometimes.

I remember a sense of frustration that prevented me from asking her to buy me something since preschool age. One day she took me to a toy shop and told me that I could choose whatever I wanted, but I was not prepared to choose anything. At that moment, I did not want anything. Perhaps it was she who wanted to buy toys, but toys were for me, and it seemed only sensible that toys were bought when I knew what I wanted. In the end, I chose an inexpensive chopping board with a half-moon with red handles.

Stuffed animals were my favorites, and she knew that. I had a few, almost as big as me, that my brother and I would use to act out stories.

But it was not just toys that caught my attention. Those were the years of an economic boom and unprecedented domestic and international trade for Italy. The years of peace following the years of war and deprivation were fertile ground for imagination and entrepreneurship. Millions of new products were invented and became available, often in a rainbow of colors that invited us to live with pleasure.

Cuteness was one of the attributes that enticed me to prefer one thing over another. That was the case of a kitchen tool used to carve little spheres out of apples or potatoes. I really wanted it, but my mother would not buy it. As an eight-year-old, I must have become cranky over it, and she got irritated. Inside myself, I came to terms with the realization that my request and my will were nothing in comparison to my mother's, and I decided that I did not want that plaything anymore out of anger and spite.

Two days later, it was time for my mother to return home from shopping. I heard her open the door and went to greet her. I saw her standing at the entrance door, with a smart-ass face, twiddling the carver. She was luring me to bite. I knew immediately what she was waiting for me to do.

My heart was full of anger at seeing how she had overstepped me and stepped up, thus forcing me to accept what I did not want anymore and say to her, "You're so good to me." But I put on a face of happiness and, hopping all the way to the entrance hall, I went "ohhh" and thanked her. People pleasing, that's what I did, and that's one instinctive action of mine that has always driven my behavior with the aim to avoid confrontation and minimize further stress and hurt to myself. I did fancy the carver, but I was never willing to pay in coins of hurt.

Ever since I was little, my mother would take me walking around the city center. We walked a lot. She did with me what her mother did with her. She walked and walked and searched all the shops to be sure that she saw all the range available in town of what she would like to buy so that she could pick exactly the type she had in her mind. Unfortunately, it was like a bottomless pit. My mother was incapable of making up her mind. If she ever ended up buying an item, she would invariably have misgivings. The only sure outcome of buying something was that she would take it back.

Her mother and Uncle's family all laughed when they heard that she had bought pajamas for my brother, had him wear them that night, and then ironed them and took them back to the shop the following day.

Growing up with a mother who could not make up her mind and just get on with things was very stressful for me. It was one thing to see relatives laugh at her attitude, but it was another to live with her indecisiveness and fastidiousness. When looking for an item of clothing for me, I had to try it on and hear her make the same requests and comments in every shop, again and again for hours. The following day, we would go back to some of the shops to try on the same things again and maybe decide. She was tired and satisfied when she could exclaim, "I have seen them all!" Sometimes she would finally buy the item after two days of the same rigmarole, and I would be happy about the new item and put it on to show Dad and Grandmother. But then it would be taken from me because she was fearful that it was the wrong choice; maybe it should have even been a different size.

Unlike my mother, I would choose something that I liked rather quickly because I knew immediately what I wanted, and I knew that I wouldn't have any regrets. But then I would find myself in one of her limited range of behaviors. She would look at me with a smiling, loving face and bright eyes that was in fact a grimace for holding back a mounting pressure inside of her. It could have been her indecisiveness, her unwillingness to spend money, or her plain and simple unwillingness to give in to my request. She would ask me if I was sure that I wanted just that and not maybe the other color or the other shape or pattern. Then I would ask her, "Maybe you don't want to buy it?"

"Yes, of course, we are going to," she would say, but she just wanted to be sure that it was the right choice, which meant choosing with your head, and not with your heart. She wanted me to choose it because it was useful or valuable or long-lasting, not because I instinctively liked it.

Sometimes I would feel my energy rain down onto the floor, and I would end up choosing something else with my brain. Other times, I would keep my initial choice. I would then look at my mother and see her with a sad smile on her face, as if she was making an effort to repress a sigh for agreeing to my choice and reaching the point of a final decision. At that point, she would ask me, "Mmm...Do you want it?" while distorting the words with a childish voice and pronunciation. My heart invariably sank because that prompt of hers made me see in a flash that nothing, absolutely nothing that we want and buy is necessary. I preferred to give up my power of choice and happiness about acquiring something new that I liked and seeing my will materialize into something pretty and fun, rather than going on playing the push-and-pull game that came so naturally to her.

When I grew up, left home, and married, I became even more aware of the weapons that money and gifts were for my mother toward me. Gifts were her way of showing how generous and unselfish she was. When she was a teenager, a Romani read her hand. Among the various traits that she saw, she stressed the "big selfishness," which could also translate into a "big ego," as we use only one term in Italian. Perhaps she spent her life disproving what that Romani saw by giving me gifts, most notably clothes and money, even against my will and requests, to the point of having me scream and beg her to not give me anything, not even a birthday gift. That's where I ended up defending myself—shortchanged. But in my youth and early married life, I accepted all that she gave me because I did not want to waste, and I knew that it would indeed be a waste if I went out and bought what I really wanted on top of what she had already given me.

I felt what was underlying her over-giving to me was what I had noticed since I was a young child: she was overriding my freedom and power of choice. It was instinctive for her to give *things* rather than what a child needs from an adult parent: guidance, advice, understanding, support, a loving presence.

When I expressed the need to have a yellow bed cover that would look nice in the bedroom, she took me to the best shop in town, where we bought a fine, pale pink fabric with little apples. Then we went to another shop to buy the trimmings, and she sewed the whole thing for me. It was her habit to buy fabrics instead of ready-made items, including when we fancied new items of clothing.

I was at my home a few days later when the doorbell rang, and I opened the door. It was my mother panting and feeling very sorry that she had bought me a pink bed cover when I wanted a yellow one. She opened the large package she was carrying, revealing what she had just bought for me. It was a beige bed cover, but she told me that there were other colors and that I could take it back to the shop and choose whatever color I wanted. So I went back to where she had bought it and picked the yellow one.

With the passing of years, I became increasingly confused about the mechanics of my asking and her complying until I asked for a tin watering can as a birthday present, and she happily gifted me a plastic one. That day, I reached the point of seriously doubting my mental sanity. I was truly worried and asked my husband with hands on my face if I perhaps had only imagined that I asked her for a tin watering can. But he reassured me.

It was so frustrating that she could not give me what I needed but would give me a lot more, thus proving what a good, generous, unselfish person she was. One day I parked the car in a large car park building across the road from where she lived. When I went to pay the charge, which amounted to about 50 cents today, I realized that I had no change in my purse. Anybody would have crossed the road and asked Mum for a coin. But I had sunk into a state of knowing that my mother would have given me what she decided, not what I needed. It was sad to know that I could not just cross the road to solve the problem. I asked the guy at the teller if he could accept a check. He was shocked, but he accepted it.

As my mother grew older, it became more and more stressful for her to imagine what I would like for a gift. It was disheartening to see that a mother did not know her daughter's tastes or wishes. Once I came to her rescue and asked her for a certain handbag of a particular shape, color, and pattern that I had seen in a particular shop, in the right-hand side window, at the intersection point of such and such coordinates. I hoped that the instructions were clear enough to single out that one bag in the whole shop. I took onto myself all the stress of the choice, hoping that my mother would be free to just go to the shop and get it.

On my birthday, she came to my home, so we could have lunch together. She brought me flowers and something else, as her usual way of presenting herself was with full hands. I was determined to just watch her and wait. We had lunch and a long chat for about three hours. Then it was time for her to go back home. She put her jacket on and put her handbag on her arm and was ready to say goodbye and take a taxi. At that point, I could not contain myself anymore. I had to ask her, "Will you or will you not give me my gift?" And so she "passed" the gift to me.

# Chapter 5

**Trigger Warning:
This chapter contains descriptions of sexual violence, which some readers may find distressing.**

My father sought a promotion at his workplace. He must have repeatedly reminded the personnel office about his request over a long time. Finally, a proposal came, and the announcement was made to me without a smile and with some worry. We would be moving to another city. I jumped with joy. I could not wait for a change. Finally, I would no longer see from my window the pediatrician's window and the crossroads where so many car accidents occurred.

The move would be gradual, with Dad going ahead alone to his new post and us following later so that we could all finish the school year. I was so excited that one day I happily told our cleaning lady about our impending move to another city. To my surprise, she was distraught. Poor woman. She was forty, and it was no longer that easy for her to find another job at such short notice. Grandmother had forbidden everybody to tell her. She should have found out only a few days before we left, not many weeks before.

It was at the end of that winter, our last in our native city, that I became a tired, and I constantly had a bit of temperature that would not go back down to normal. There was only one solution: let's go and see the pediatrician. Before diagnosing me, she needed a blood test. That would be my first blood test ever. As the nurse prepared my arm, my mother took my face in her hands so that I would not turn my head and look. I could never forget her inability to conceal her anxiety behind her forced half-smile.

When the results came, she and the doctor talked in private. Then I saw my mother standing in front of me, her feet close together, her upper body slightly tilted forward. She was jiggling her knees like embarrassed young children do. "Anna, listen! Now you are a grown child, and you are going to have injections." My heart and eyes burst into a stream of tears, and I left.

The morning that the course was supposed to start, I pretended I could not get up from bed. My mother endeavored to make as much noise as possible when entering my room and rolling up the blind. The janitor of our block of flats came to give me the injection. She was the injector for many blocks of flats on the street and knew everything about everybody's health, treatments, and buttocks, and she would tell everybody all about it.

My mother assisted. I screamed and sobbed in rage, frustration, and humiliation. She attempted to tell me to stop, but the janitor kindly said to let me be and let off steam. I walked with a stiff leg, from my waist down, for days. My mother never believed that injecting penicillin powder into a buttock was shockingly painful.

During the spring, my mother and I took the train to visit Dad in Trieste, the city to which we would be moving. Dad was happy to see us and to see me. He took us around to visit the city and to the fish restaurants. I tasted fish like I had never had before. We breathed an air of novelty, of change, of holiday. We were hopeful that the move would be a happy one and were full of excitement with new places to discover and new habits to take on. My parents were appreciative of the orderly city and of the disposition of its inhabitants, who were inclined to enjoy life in the open air with wit and laughter. That was one of the happiest weeks of my life. It was a present that made me forget the life I dropped the moment I stepped on the train.

When departure day came, all that I had forgotten reared its ugly head again. I was at the station, and I was crying a river, with my heart cut deeply at the thought of going back to injections, Grandmother, school, and Mother's haughty, watchful eye. I held onto Dad, who exclaimed, "Don't cry like that.

You'll make me cry too!" He said so twice. Then Mother and I boarded the train, and I resigned myself to my fate. I cried silently but profusely for hours, sitting in my seat in front of my mother, who looked out of the window all the time.

Forty years on, it dawned on me that it was reasonable to think that some passengers may have thought, *Why doesn't that mother do something?* But it was only fifty years later that I realized that Dad was, indeed, crying with me.

I had those injections till the end of the summer when my mother chose not to give me the last one because I made too much fuss every time. She said so with anger, haughtiness, and bitter regret for the renunciation of her right over her own daughter—which I, the rightless one, had forced on her—as well as a hint of her generosity for which I should be overtly thankful.

A few years later, she told a doctor that I had had that particular medical treatment. That fifty-year-old doctor was startled and fearful of how painful those injections were. Looking at him, my mother's eyes and mouth opened slowly in amazement. She did not comment, but she took that information into her memory as a weapon that she would use against me in years to come.

Before moving to the new city, it was necessary to find a home. So we left in the summer and temporarily stayed at the hotel where my father was staying. Dad was working, so Mother looked for a flat, with me trailing after her.

It was like going to shops to try on clothes. It was an endless quest for something that never met expectations. Not only was I exhausted from walking, but I also felt more and more disheartened for having to give up my usual summer life. I was walking endlessly beside my mother, while my seventeen-year-old brother was having a holiday on his own in the countryside resort we stayed at regularly every year and liked so much.

In any case, Dad was planning to live there only until his retirement, which would be thirteen years later. Although it may seem like a long time, he was determined to rent a flat and not buy one. Moreover, he insisted that we live on one of the main streets in the city center, and we settled for a flat on the second floor.

I began to feel increasing distress for the growing, subtle disappointment that my parents fell into. My mother could not teach; she had to stay at home and wait for an opening in the local school system. My father realized that he had been used as a pawn to get rid of someone who was misbehaving and could not have been fired in any other way. In addition, my brother was furious for being taken away from his friends and comfort zone. In general, we were like immigrants in this city whose culture and traditions were very different from what we were accustomed to. We needed to learn to adjust, yet felt clearly unwelcome at times due to political and financial reasons beyond us.

Getting up in the morning, my mother would have a view of our next-door neighbor shaving, exposing the wound of an amputated arm at the shoulder joint. She cried constantly with outrage of falling so low as to overlook that inner dusty courtyard, while she had grown up overlooking a large, pretty garden and the shimmering sea. There were rats in the kitchen. On top of everything, my grandmother died within a year, and my mother had to begin cooking for us.

In our general effort to settle and fit in, appreciate the local ways of living, and start making acquaintances, my father made it crystal clear that I must never take on the local accent.

I was placed in the school near our home, with a teacher several people had told my mother was the best.

I took in every sensation and feeling and kept it inside, only for myself. There was no way that I would be taken into consideration by grown-ups who were so burdened and preoccupied. There was no room for me, for my needs. I had learned by experience that I was thought to overreact, so I had better hide my true feelings. A subtle realization at the back of my mind told me that my parents were not able to help or include me in moving through this transition together. I just went on obeying, step after step, like sheep do. But I began not to smile.

My brother, with his attitude of having been wronged, commanded attention from my mother, who snapped to look at and listen to him, whatever she was doing, including while doing something with me. She was nervous about his requests, though deep down, she enjoyed having to deal with him and his attitude of reproach, which she found intelligent and humorous.

I was critical of my brother's attitude. I was more easygoing, which meant I was never a priority. What I had or needed or wanted to say was unimportant and dropped. As a creative countermeasure, I made a cardboard sign, like the ones that police pull out to stop cars, with a white handle and round head and the red disk, and I wrote, "Stop yapping" around the white rim. My mother laughed and found it very funny. That was all.

The concoction of heavy energy within me settled and took residence. I went to school every day with the obedience of a good girl, forcing myself to believe that I must be as good as my classmates were. I tried to take no notice of the muffled inner scream of fear that, with time, took on the form of anxiety in my tummy and jagged, frozen breathing and speaking.

The teacher did not relent for one single second from her overpowering, scowling attitude about our obedience and performance. In the year I spent facing her verbal and nonverbal language, I became anxious and fearful of making mistakes in assignments and homework. In addition, I could not understand how such a reputedly good teacher could not speak with the same correctness of language with which I had grown up and would use expressions that were taken from the local dialect or the other languages that were spoken in this city on the border. I assumed by her twenty-year-old clothes that she was not prepared to spend money and make herself, if not pretty, at least tastefully dressed. But most of all, she blatantly smiled and gave good marks to the majority of middle-class pupils, while she was stern with and even critical of lower-class pupils.

I happened to see her a couple of years later. She did not recognize me. She said with some disappointment, "I remembered you taller." I thought I was the only one who was not comfortable in class. Twenty or thirty years on, I found out that the "best teacher" caused insomnia in classmates, and some remembered her as "terrible."

A bit of respite came with middle school. The choice was between the state school in the neighborhood or a private school. Having seen the entrance door of the state school, my mother was repelled. The entrance was on a heavily trafficked two-lane street, and the only protection for the children was a three-meter railing on the edge of the narrow pavement. In addition, the renown of that school was not among the best in town.

My mother talked with the mother of a family that, like us, had moved to this city and was living two doors from us. She said that her daughter had gone to state school, but she was unhappy and even had some unwanted effects that today we would call somatization. She, therefore, moved her daughter, who was one year older than me, to the private school run by nuns that was about fifteen minutes by car from our home.

I was enrolled in the nun-run middle school. It was beautiful, with a large mature garden and a yard where the children could run, play, and have a snack during mid-morning break. It was even possible for us pupils to wait for our parents to pick us up after the end of lessons under the surveillance of one of the nuns. This was my case until I was permitted to walk alone to and from school.

On my fourteenth birthday, my father gave me a beautiful silver keyring from which the key to our flat was dangling. I was growing and becoming autonomous, thus freeing my elders from the time constraints of ferrying me to and from school. So, I would open the door by myself to an empty home.

I have heard from lots of sides that nuns can be nasty, but that was never my experience. They were teachers, and I did not find any difference between their personalities and the personalities of lay teachers, except that they mentioned the Lord and Christ more often. There was one nun, however, who was prone to criticizing teenage girls.

She was the main teacher, meaning that she taught Italian, history, and Latin, which made up a large portion of our curriculum. Lots of girls who were growing faster than me and looked like young women just shrugged their shoulders and scoffed. But I was not like them. I looked at them, and they seemed a million miles from me.

One day that teacher tested me, and I failed. I was enraged and frustrated for sensing that I was incapable of standing my ground, showing some pride, and demanding a bit of respect. I also felt my uncontrollable programming to submit close like a firewall, as I had been trained to do with my parents and my grandmother since an early age. I went to my desk and cried, sobbing in frustration. At the end of the lesson, I heard her come and call me, while an understanding classmate said to her kindly, "Leave her alone. She is not used to getting bad marks."

*What do they know?*

All in all, I had a good time there. At some point, I even felt a sincere inclination to become a nun one day and told my parents. "Yeah, right," my dad said with some amusement at my announcement.

Ironically, my brother and I were enrolled in religious schools even though my father was biased against priests and nuns and the church in general. However, my mother was very religious, took us to mass every Sunday, and knew all the prayers in Latin, including those that only the officiating priest would recite. She was observant of religious precepts too. She made sure that we ate fish on Fridays and resisted the temptation to nibble sweet goodies for the purpose of practicing sacrifice.

In the beginning of a Catholic mass, there is a point where the priest announces: "Let us acknowledge our sins," and then he pauses in silence for a few seconds to allow the congregation to review their sins.

I could only think of one sin for myself—the sin of pride that I had no sins at all.

## Chapter 6

The time came for me to go to high school. That was the same state school my brother had attended for the last two years before going on to study medicine at the local university. There was no question that I should take on classical studies. Which high school I should attend was never a subject of discussion. Anyway, it was my only chance to pursue university studies in archaeology, which I had been passionate about since I was very young.

In the new class, I saw small groups of classmates who were already friends from being together at middle school. I was alone like many others. I felt lost in a crowd.

Those were years of intense inner transformation for me, and all the while I felt hindered by those waves of energy moving within me. They were preventing me from being happy about going to school like several classmates seemed to be. I felt depressed all the time, with an inclination to sadness and a need to cry. I spent afternoons in my room, listening to classical music and sensing its currents with full intensity.

In addition, my monthly periods became rather painful on the first day, but my mother did not want me to take any medication for it. That was odd. After forcing chemicals into my body without ever considering possible ill side effects, she now did not want me to take a painkiller once in a while.

My first period had come four years earlier, when I was ten. The day I saw blood, I did not know what was happening. I knew I had to tell my mother, but I also knew that I needed to buffer myself from her reaction, so

I decided to act nonchalant. To my surprise, she sat down on my bed and talked to me, lifting one eyebrow occasionally, explaining that it eventually happens to girls. "You have become a 'young lady'," she announced, adding to keep it absolutely quiet and never mention it to anybody, especially Dad, my brother, and all men and boys in general.

I understood that having periods had to be a well-guarded secret, but I soon realized that it was one within a huge number of people. Regardless, that secret had a connotation of uncleanness and uneasiness, and it was nothing to be particularly happy about. When we schoolgirls had our periods and did not feel well enough to participate in exercises at the gym, we would say that we were "indisposed." Female schoolmates would look closely and straight into the eyes of another schoolmate and whisper, "Are you already a 'young lady'?"

I could not perform well enough in high school, which was very frustrating. Why couldn't I let a flow of words out of my mouth or pen like my best classmates did, repeating what they had learned? What was so difficult for me? The only answer that I could find was that I needed to change my studying method. Maybe study more diligently than I had done before. *Come on, make another effort, and the teacher will change her opinion of you.* Yes, she did, but not without sarcasm, as if it was by pure chance that I had a sudden, albeit short-lived, spike of intelligence.

I was constantly in inner turmoil, which made me feel so much lower than anybody else. "Your early teens are the happiest time of your life," some middle-aged woman said to me. But I was inherently incapable of making it the best time of my life, which made me angry with myself. I saw classmates laughing together while I was only feeling the need to withdraw—and not just from school. Walking alone on the street, I felt the urge to walk straight ahead quickly, with no distractions or window shopping, and reach the safety of home, so I could slam the door behind me with a sigh of relief. I walked in a bubble of defense, so fragile that anybody and anything could breach it just with a look or a word. I felt safe only in my world, which was the size of my bedroom.

At night, I would wake up with a terrible sensation of shame in my guts.

I made it a habit to review the past day, what I had done, what had happened, and how I reacted. Consistently, I concluded that I had nothing of which to be ashamed. Then I would turn to the other side and go back to sleep.

When the time to wake up was getting near, the anxiety of hearing the alarm clock bursting as if I were at the firehouse caused disrupted sleep, tiredness, a fast heart rate, and a discharge of cortisol. It was a terrible way to wake up. But luckily, more humane clocks were invented, and my father gave me one that played a happy tune. It was better, but it was still an alarm clock prodding me to go to school.

* * *

In those years, I experienced the deep emotional importance that food had for me. After I started school, I lost the habit of having breakfast at home, I guess for lack of time or because my stomach was still asleep. I had a snack mid-morning, during the break between lessons, which I would buy from the vending machine.

In middle school, I would walk back home and find my father there. He had his problems at work and an air of disillusion about him. He asked me to set the table in that dark kitchen while he fixed lunch, and we waited for Mum and my brother to come back home. That was hardly the atmosphere I needed to come home to. Mother was teaching in the morning and sometimes went out of her way to prepare something before she left. But that food was full of her feelings toward the situation she found herself in: *I don't know what to do. I don't know what I'm doing. I hate doing this. I used to have two maids.*

A few years later, she was given the afternoon shift, which meant that she had time to breathe and think in the mornings. Meanwhile, we had moved to a larger, more prestigious flat up the street. My room was the last along the corridor, next to the kitchen and the laundry room, while the master bedroom and my brother's room were near the entrance hall. My brother had a toilet closet all to himself, opposite his bedroom door.

The mornings at school became longer as the years progressed and more lessons piled up. The walk home from high school took me nearly half an hour, so I usually reached home around 1:30 p.m. I was ravenous, but I clearly needed emotional nourishment more than food. I would get home, turn the key in the lock, open the door and…smell lunch ready. So many times, that smell alone would trigger tears in my eyes and a knot in my throat, which became so easily undone that I had to make a dash to the bathroom and lock myself in and cry a stream of tears, while thinking, *Thank you, Mum. Thank you for cooking!*

I could not show myself in that state to anyone. What would they have thought of me? I would have been interrogated and dismissed as ridiculous. I knew very well that I must keep my feelings to myself if I wanted to dodge further hurt.

My classmate who sat next to me sometimes would show me the sandwich that her mother prepared for her snack every day. She would notice with glee that her mother added an olive or a sweet chili. I felt her mother's care for her in preparing a sandwich that would not only be natural and nourishing but also would enclose a little surprise of extra goodness. Like a wink from Mum to her child.

*Her mother can do that because she is a housewife and has time to take care of her three children,* I thought logically. *My mother cannot do that; she works. She cannot do everything. That is understandable, and I cannot have everything.*

I took after my father. He received pleasure from eating, and so did I. We would enjoy our full lunches at the restaurant on Sundays. He ate with an appetite, more than he would have wanted to. He had a tendency to put on weight and was careful not to overeat because he knew it was not good for his health. That idea made him eat lunch and dinner avidly and quickly, jump up from his chair still munching, and rush to the sitting room where he had his cigarettes.

My father often remarked to me with a smile, "Ah, you're nourishing yourself!" when I managed a full meal at the restaurant. It was so good! It was so different from the staple spaghetti and steak we had at home every single day. But I also perceived a subtle hint that he was saying that perhaps I was costing him money. And then there was always my brother's humor about me eating all the time, and my mother after him with an impersonation of a cartoon me with bigger and bigger buttocks.

I was still chuckling at their ways of making fun of my habits. However, they were habits that I could not help—a good appetite and listening to some particular kinds of music again and again. They were a kind of refuge for me. Perhaps I should have been more careful about making my preferences known. I got hurt when I was passionate about something, and people around me mocked me. I felt ashamed for being unable to help liking something that others did not like and for which they might even criticize me.

I internalized that what I liked—for example, folk music—was unbecoming for the status of us as a family. Both my mother and brother, in their behavior and words, conveyed their deliberate choice of what was elegant and distinguished. Anything that did not live up to those standards was snubbed as "vulgar."

Mum and Dad had very good taste by Italian standards. We could not afford expensive clothes, nor did we want any, but the quality of the fabrics and their patterns was always selected carefully. From them, I learned good taste in clothing, including matching colors, and in furnishing the home.

Dad worked for a shipping company that had only passenger ships in those days. He was in charge of selecting goods that would be sold at the boutiques on board, and the first class of passenger ships required top-notch service and goods.

We were an average middle-class family like my grandparents had been before us. The economic boom we were living in allowed my dad to invest some money occasionally in safe-haven assets and in affordable antiques that he loved so much. It was so that our apartment was tastefully furnished and looked as if we had heirlooms from grandparents. Dad could not stand it when the cleaning lady dusted those antique pieces. He insisted that they must look antique. He did not make the distinction between dirty and old.

Mother was squeamish. She had the tendency to rinse things many times over, which she kept doing throughout her life. In particular, she would wash and rinse the foods that were to be eaten raw, such as fruit and some vegetables. One day I helped wash grapes, but she snatched the bowl from me in disapproval and kept rinsing until almost all the grapes became detached from their little stalks. That was the way I learned to wash grapes so they were safe to eat, and I continued to do that, including one day when we had a cousin come for dinner. My mother looked down at me and said, "Is this the way to wash grapes?"

I looked at my mother in shock, but I did not say anything. Our cousin looked at me and, with a sigh, showed me clearly that he was making an effort to eat the grapes that had been served to him that way. I knew consciously and logically that my mother said that on purpose. But I could not believe in my heart that she was capable of treating me like a fairy-tale stepmother would.

* * *

Eventually, my mother had her teaching job moved to the morning, so she could spend the afternoon seeing to the running of the household. We had a cleaning lady who dusted and cleaned the bathroom and kitchen, but there was still a lot left to do, such as the wash and ironing. I could see my mother at work in the laundry room from my bedroom across the hall. I remember her grossed-out face looking down at the clothes and handkerchiefs she was removing stains from before putting them into the washing machine. I was a young teenager and downhearted at seeing my mother so incapable of feeling and looking normal. I didn't understand why she didn't just do the chore and maybe comment about it later to let off some steam.

That chore, in particular, may have been repulsive to her, but she could also be frantic and frazzled about food shopping and planning what to prepare for my brother's lunch and snacks. My father helped in the kitchen with cooking and loading the dishwasher, but it seemed that no help was enough to ease her high electric charge.

I may have been selfish, but her attitude just repelled me, and I never approached her to try and soothe her. I could not get over the need to defend myself from her projecting emotional sparks.

With time, I learned what was going on inside her. I realized that she had not changed at all from those days when I was nine and I happened to be in a hotel room where she was having a row with my sixteen-year-old brother, who did not know what to do with her. She was crying and kneeling and furiously whispering sorry to him with the intent to show him how unfairly he was twisting things around. They were oblivious to my presence and certainly unaware of the emotional wound that was opened in my heart by witnessing their push and pull. I was crying too, but they did not notice me in the corner. I was shouting inside me, *Don't suffer like that, Mum, I will suffer for you!*

That cry had the power of a vow and stayed in my soul. Hidden in the darkness of my soul's caves was the obligation to pay a high toll for being born and growing. No matter how unfair it seemed to be, I was a daughter, and I had to pay to exist in terms of my energy, happiness, will, and choices, both present and future, and turn the past into broken pieces to cry about and hopefully forget.

My mother needed a long holiday, as all mothers do. She was frazzled but proud of her busyness and juggling with work and family. She spoke of her housewife friends as "extremely busy" with their children, which left me wondering what life for her was like with a job on top. Such remarks forced me to squeeze my brains and muscles and double my efforts to make her life as easy as possible. That realization made me aware that up to that point, I had not done enough and there was so much more I could do.

I did help my mother with house chores, as every good daughter should do. I helped her prepare lunch and iron the linen. But I preferred wearing clothes longer than I should have and putting a drop of perfume on my shirts so that I could wear them for another two or three days, rather than giving her too much washing to do. I began using paper handkerchiefs when she decided she was done with cotton ones, while my brother had no reaction to my mother's request and continued using cloth ones.

My brother sometimes acted as a third parent to me, telling me off because I did not help our overworked mother enough. He could not understand at all why I was so stubborn and never did things the easy way, as if I were ramming the wall open instead of passing through the doorway, half a meter to the side. "Anna, why do you do that?" he would ask me. It was hard for me to see that my viewpoint and energy were not taken into due consideration. I had to do what I was told to do, and I naturally reacted in anger and frustration.

Music was my escape, my wings, the air for my breath, the colors for my soul. I became passionate about opera. I already knew bits and pieces of famous arias, but seeing a whole opera performed at the theater introduced me to a world of classical music that was way more enticing than chamber or symphonic music or even pop music. I bought records. I learned the lyrics and listened to operas on the radio. I shared what I was discovering and learning with my mother. She had to hold her belly with laughter at the lyrics and the choice of words and rhymes.

In the end, I made up my mind. "I want to become an opera singer," I told her.

She burst out with the loudest ha-ha laughter that she had ever done, with her mouth wide open, all the while looking at me. *Yet another one of her crazy ideas,* she must have thought. Father's reaction was different. I saw his health worsening at the news. My parents, especially my father, were horribly embarrassed that I wanted to study singing. They were convinced to the core that music was for those youngsters who failed at school because of their poor levels of intelligence. Funny…where does that leave famous concert musicians, then? Were they thick? Really?

But singing apparently was the worst of all musical performances, according to them. And a woman who opens her mouth.… They were lost for words. Sopranos have always been mocked for being oversized, and I am small. Their mouths gape ridiculously, and I have a small mouth that my mother likes so much. Learning how to sing opera is almost like torture. What is the use of learning opera in the late twentieth century?

But despite all they said, I was passionate about it. I took the entrance exam at the Conservatory and passed it. My parents were embarrassed to the point of hiding. "Don't tell anyone!" whispered my mother, doubling each consonant. So I did not tell anyone except one classmate who was studying piano at the Conservatory.

## PART I: THAT'S LIFE

One day, my father came back home. He had run into a friend of his to whom he confessed his worries about me studying singing at the Conservatory. His jaw was still dropped when he told us what his friend had said to him. "That is so good! You must encourage her!" He could not believe it.

## Chapter 7

My father convinced me that abandoning school was a bad idea. I was sixteen, struggling and suffering so much that I could not go on. He insisted gently and persuasively that I should go on because a qualification is useful later in life. So I did, but that school was such a burden on my soul that I developed the thought that even if I lost a child, that pain would never match how much I suffered at high school.

One day I made the colossal mistake of saying that to him, he who had lost his younger brother at war. Now I appreciate that expressing those feelings to Dad was inappropriate. But it was not inappropriate to express the fullness of my suffering for having to attend that school against my will and energy every day. I went every morning, for five years, with big written and oral tests at the end of it. My father's gesture in reaction to what I said was one more sign that I was way too sensitive and wrong. Swiftly raising one arm and averting his face, his actions meant, *This is too much. You don't know what you're talking about.*

I should have kept my mouth shut and avoided adding to my suffering. That was one more lesson that my problems were nothing in comparison to other people's problems.

I did not do that badly at school. After all, I had reasonably good marks. But it took great effort to counteract my soul's need to expand. My emotions needed to find safety and dialogue instead of risk and criticism, and my body needed to move instead of being tied to a chair for six hours a day and ending up feeling cold. I needed to elicit and educate what was inside of me instead of being lectured about subject matters that were suitable for PhD studies, and then getting ranked. This consumed a huge amount of my energy and made me confused as to what life was and would be in the future. The shy need of my soul was to study what I felt I had a flair for.

I knew that there was something wrong with the way I was forced and forcing myself to live. The demands that were put on me as a teenager were many, such as: being happy in general and to go to school, performing well at school, being full of energy, and having friends, not to mention being happy to have a boyfriend and accepting physical interaction. These demands were so pressing that I wanted to run as fast as I could out of youth. However, there was something very wrong with that. I was living my youth just restlessly, fidgeting to become an adult.

My mother saw that I was not good at certain subjects. She was particularly keen to have me learn how to write good compositions. My teachers said that my test essays were short and confused. I was completely lost. I did not know what to do or what they wanted from me. Ideas just did not come to my mind.

I asked a classmate if I could read her essay that was marked rather high, and I discovered that she said absolutely nothing over those three or four pages, but she said nothing with ease, flow, and eloquence. I was shocked. I thought that I had to get a genius idea and expound on it because that would be the only time that I would have something to say that would be appreciated. The request of school and life was that everybody must have an opinion about everything, and when the teacher proposes a topic, a button must light up your brain and a stream of sentences must flow out of your hands and onto the pages. I watched how my classmates jumped into action when the teacher announced the title of an essay. No sooner had she stopped speaking, and they already had their heads bent over the blank pages as their brains sparked with a torrent of things to say, and they immediately started writing. And kept writing. No one had to think about what to say. I was still watching them, with no ideas coming to my mind.

My mother told me how much she admired writers and their

high-sounding sentences and recherché terms. I knew that her celebrated letters to her uncle's family gathered an audience. However, I never quite knew how she had done at writing essays at school, but she must have been better than I was—even the time that her teacher remarked, "You beat the bass drum too much."

She taught me that an essay needs to start and then expand and grow more and then taper out. Actually, she told me all that in onomatopoeic sounds and shaky hand movements, at the sight of which I complied with a giggle.

Soon after, on my birthday, I found my mother's wrapped present waiting for me at the lunch table next to my plate—two books on how to write essays. My heart sank, and so did my energy levels. I was a teenager and felt misunderstood. That was not the kind of support that I needed.

Around that time, the teacher gave us a test essay in class. I kept staring at the blank pages, which kept staring back at me with a blank look, in a power struggle for who stayed blank longer. After a while, a long while, I could not take it anymore. I asked the teacher if I could go out for a moment and did not come back. I went to see the secretary and told her why I was so nervous and emotional. She took me to the medical room where I could lie down and spend the rest of the hours assigned to writing the essay.

When I reemerged, I saw my classmates in a panic. They told me I had given them a fright and that they feared that something bad had happened to me. I could not believe that they cared. At home, Mother was worried about my performance. She went to speak with the teacher, who was very understanding and knew well what was going on inside of me. He said I should rest assured he would not count that as a fail.

It was much worse with the philosophy teacher. I noticed again and again that he would get impatient and ask complicated questions to students who, like me, were shorter than 1.65 meters (5 feet four inches); however, I seriously doubt that anybody else ever noticed what was so palpable to me. Everybody who was taller than that seemed to be doing much better at his subject matter and were asked easy questions.

I was so disoriented by his confounding attitude that my mind would go blank, and I could not open my mouth. He was known to be the toughest teacher in the school, and philosophy was the toughest subject. The truth was if he had taught differently, more students would have understood.

A girl student, who was shorter than I was, told me that the philosophy teacher had said to her, "I do not like you." To which she replied, "It is reciprocal!" She was annoyed but not to the point of being angry. She had no qualms in retorting the words of that authority figure, and she did not feel put down by him at all. But I was not like her. I was almost shocked that a student would have the impudence to answer back, no matter how inappropriate what the teacher had said was.

I spent hours crying in frustration in my bedroom, raging and venting my spleen against that teacher. My mother saw what was going on and dismissed the whole thing as me not doing well at philosophy. But that was the only teacher she sent my father to talk to. She would go and speak with any other teacher except him.

After another poor oral test, at the end of which he even mocked me as if I was a crybaby, I went home and developed the idea of taking matters into my own hands. The following day, I approached him in the corridor and said, "There is something very wrong in our relationship." He looked at me from his lanky height through his glasses that made his eyes as small as pinheads, but through those thick lenses, I could see that his eyes had opened wide in amazement. From that day on, his attitude toward me changed for the better.

The trauma of having to deal with someone like him lingered unresolved within me for decades. It was no use knowing how he had suffered in his life before I met him. The forgetfulness that time spread over my bad memories was thin indeed and was just waiting to be ripped open when I was ready, or not, to finally get him out of my system. Not one but two triggers appeared in my life at times close together to revive that unresolved issue to the red-hot point in my guts. I was prey to demons for days on end and had tormented sleep. It took some hefty and extended forgiveness work to find some emotional balance again.

\* \* \*

In the spring of the fifth school year, the final exam was approaching. The teachers wanted to know what each of us intended to do or study after school was over. I said that I wanted to continue my music studies at the Conservatory. Both the Italian teacher and the philosophy teacher were amazed. What a surprise that little unassuming Anna was studying to become an opera singer. I was still conditioned by the shame that my parents had attached to my music studies, so I was unable to take in their pride for me that was evident from their expression and voice.

However, my performance as a singing student became increasingly poor, and I became frustrated at my efforts that amounted to nothing, if not worsening. I did not understand why my voice was small, and my throat could not find the right form to let out sounds like opera singers do. My voice did not "run" as big operatic voices have to in order to reach the recesses of a theater. My throat was tight.

At the end of the academic year, one month before the final exam at high school, I failed the exam at the Conservatory. That meant I would not be accepted to study there anymore. If I wanted to pursue my studies further, I could only take private lessons and register for the Conservatory's final exam.

My mother was overjoyed and exclaimed, "Destiny is leading you by the hand!" plus one of her Latin sentences, *Carmina non dant panem*—that is, poetry cannot feed you. As for Dad, I perceived that he drew a sigh of relief and even seemed to have a health improvement. I read between the lines that they were happy about my failure. Now I got it—I must fail at what I like in order to make my parents happy, and keep failing to keep them happy.

I had thought that following a dream would lead to happiness, but I was naive as to what was needed in order to materialize that dream. I would have needed to practice, practice, practice. I would have needed talent, and my mother repeated to me that "we are not for music." And yet, both the guitar teacher a few years back and one of the singing teachers had said to me that I did have what was needed to build on. But my father scoffed—he knew all too well that was their way to get money out of him.

I compared myself to other people I had heard of who got their certificates from the Conservatory as opera singers but instead pursued careers in their university studies. They did it. Why had I failed? I was gripped by a depressing shame, as if my soul had been battered to the point of making me understand once and for all that my dreams were airy-fairy whims, my requests were fanciful, and that I was different and less-than.

Many years later, I heard from various sources that my singing teacher was notorious for ruining voices. So it was not entirely my fault, after all. But that failure of mine was the biggest stain and pain in my soul's CV for decades.

To tell the truth, I was very shy about singing in front of the public. I did dream of performing on stage, but I would have had to overcome the fear of being heard. No matter how much I wanted and needed to be heard, to have a voice, I was very fearful of criticism. But I thought, speaking and writing aside, *Perhaps if I sing loudly, beautifully, and melodiously, I will be heard and listened to and what I say will be accepted.*

However, of one thing I was always absolutely sure—*I would never want my parents to be among the public.*

\* \* \*

Like my father before he married, I liked gambling. I gambled at my final exam by choosing subject matters that no one else had chosen, and that is something I would do all my life. I do what no one else will do, just because it is there waiting to be done. I did not know what it meant "to play to one's own strengths." All my life, I had been conditioned to strive, so I thought that exams should also be a battle, not just a walk. Perhaps my classmates had talked with their parents about selecting the subject matters they felt confident about. Not me. School was my own business, my own burden and problem. Besides, I might not have been the type of daughter that parents could easily advise. So I gambled on my own.

The final exam was terrible on my nervous system. I performed poorly.

The news of the marks reached me and my mother when we were visiting her mother and brother's family. I was chatting with my cousin when she flung the bedroom door open. She was hysterically happy, red in her cheeks and the tip of her nose, and her voice was almost raucous with excitement. "I cannot believe it!" she kept repeating, alternating that with some sounds that carried the energy of "what an achievement!" I had passed with a mark two points higher than the lowest.

I knew I had given my parents doubts about my performance and success at school. However, what they never saw was the extent of the hellish struggle that I put up with relationships and with myself for pushing against my nature and will. And there she was, overjoyed for my overachievement that equated with a barely missed fail. *So that's what they have always thought of me.* It was depressing.

A few years ago, I happened to hear the news that two girls had committed suicide after failing their school year. The reporter commented on the way young people react to life nowadays, taking extreme measures even as a consequence for something as silly as failing a school year.

Hey, where did that reporter live? Or rather, I should say, *how* did that reporter live? Different from me, for sure. I could empathize with those two poor teenagers perfectly well.

The effects of the double failure, both at the Conservatory and at high school, and of my parents' reaction to them was so heavy and depressing on my heart and emotions that I could not contain myself. I sat in front of my mother and my aunt, and I expressed my deep sadness. I cried and poured my heart out, telling them that I saw Dad's health worsening by my choice to study singing.

They were sitting on the sofa in front of me, and all they did throughout my jittery, choking sobbing was to pity me by tilting their heads at me, uttering sounds, and looking at each other in disbelief. They were at a loss for words at how much I had misconstrued reality. Perhaps in my sorrowful state, I would not have accepted to be hugged. But at that moment, I needed understanding, guidance, and togetherness. None of that was ever available in the family. Seeing the two of them reacting that way to how I felt and expressed myself made me feel even worse.

That is the risk that people like me run when we reach the boiling-over level, and we cannot help speaking out. We are seen as overreacting and misconstruing, even unjust sometimes. Others shake their heads and don't know what to do with us. The solution that I adopted from then on was to hold back and repress my emotions that would normally have the power of a volcanic eruption until they calmed down and I could speak in a balanced way. That might take me years. And that is not healthy for me, I know.

I continued my singing by taking private lessons that I paid for myself out of the pocket money that Dad gave me every month. But inflation went up in those years of the oil crisis, and no money was left for me. I asked for a raise, and Dad gave me a bit more, but his silent nonverbal expression made me understand that it was an effort for him to give me that extra bit, as if he was not entirely happy with how I was spending it. However, I would not spend it that way for long. Eventually, my singing teacher left the city and sought her career elsewhere. That was the end of my opera singing but not of the emotions and feelings attached to it, including a lingering jealousy for all those who made it to the stage, especially the mediocre ones.

## Chapter 8

While I was going to high school, I reached the age when one becomes interested in one friend in particular, which in my case was of the opposite sex. But the upbringing I had, the education I received, and most certainly the atmosphere that I felt at home, plus my obedience to rules of good behavior—all kept me as naive as a damsel.

One day, a cousin of mine visited. She, my mother, and I happened to be talking together. Our conversation revolved around gynecologists, and my mother said that they used their little fingers to examine little girls. I said something that gave away my ignorance, at which point my mother put up an air of superior surprise and remarked, "Oh, Anna, then you are an ingénue!" My younger cousin looked at me with a smile and look that showed all her knowledge of the matter.

It was common for my mother to put me on the spot in the presence of guests. It happened many times, on different occasions, and for different reasons. I instantly felt sorrowful with hurt. I was ashamed for being stupid and to have never seen it coming, ashamed for not knowing what I had never been taught, and very confused for having followed Mother's upbringing strictly and being implicitly expected by her to break the rules secretly. However, it was impossible that my mother would put me on the spot purposefully. An ever-smiling mother meant no ill to me. It was I who became offended when she, who was so witty, involved me in her fun. I felt so incapable of laughing and being easygoing and so hated myself for being touchy and so daft as to never, ever see it coming.

I did have boyfriends. I appreciate that parents have good reasons for keeping an eye on whom their children go out with, and my parents were no exception. However, I felt that my mother's eyes knew everything about what I was thinking, doing, hiding. Yes, I had to hide some parts of me. I needed to safeguard some independence, or I would have felt totally exposed to her sidelong, suspecting look. It was like having her as a probe inside of me.

She asked questions about my boyfriends, commented on them, and sometimes gave them nicknames that she would pronounce in a funny way. My upbringing forced me to answer questions as fully as possible with complete sincerity. My mother once said, "My children never lie." It was true. I was incapable of lying. When asked about someone or something, I answered with all I knew; maybe not all at once, but in a sequence of increasingly appeasing information to pacify her inevitable electric reactions, such as worry.

Some people have fond memories of their youth's love. I don't. I regard all my boyfriends as mistakes that I attracted into my life through the energies that were battling inside of me. The first left me soon, and so did the third. The second one was boring and wanted to dominate me as his mother was dominating him; another one was impotent, but at least he was an intellectual, while another was a sort of sex addict.

All the while, I had to keep complying with the rule set by my father to be home by 9:00 p.m., which was extended to 10:00 p.m. when I was studying at university. This compounded with mother's hailstorm of worried, energetic instructions to be careful and to not do this and not do that. Unlike all my friends, especially the boys, the ensuing effect was that I could not relax and have fun.

My father was particularly fearful of something bad happening to me. He told me not to go to dark places and to be very circumspect. He expressed his worry to me about the trafficking of white women for sexual slavery. He talked with sincere fear and sorrow about the killing of innocent girls who were found dead and naked in remote places. It was clear to me that he did not want something like that to ever happen to me. But I cannot help thinking that if anything of that sort had ever occurred to me, he would have been distraught by the loss of me but also incapable of managing the shame of having a lascivious daughter.

His mother thanked God she never had daughters, or Grandfather would have walked on the street in front of them wielding a sword.

One day, when the two of us were alone at home, Dad came and talked to me from behind me, broaching the subject matter of my boyfriend. Then he hugged me and burst into tears at the prospect of my marrying and leaving home. "You are always my little girl!" he said. I did not know what to do. I just stretched my arm backward and caressed his head.

Every evening that I went out, I had to tell him when I would return home. I would find him sitting in his armchair, smoking, maybe watching TV or reading the newspaper. His habit originated from an episode that happened a few years before. My parents were acquainted with a gentleman who had a single son. The loving father would wait for his young adult son to come back home at night, whatever the time. He would sit in his armchair and wait, and only after his son had returned home would he go to bed. My parents were shocked when they heard the news that the son had died in a car accident.

So, what else could I think of other than that my father was fearful that I would die at night and that only after I came back home would he draw a sigh of relief? Having him stay awake waiting for me signaled to me that I was responsible for my father's well-being and had to restrict my freedom and independence. In addition, it was clear that my parents did not trust me. In fact, they were not free to trust me. Their way of being protective of me was to be commanded by their own fears.

I was in my early twenties when I told my mother how I felt, obviously while crying, in comparison to my friends who were all feeling freer to enjoy their time at that age. She told Dad, and finally, I found them asleep when I returned.

My mother guarded me against behaving like she did when she wept while writing letters to her beloved, who eventually orchestrated a situation whereby she would casually find out that it was her "destiny" to be abandoned. Thirty years on, she was still bitter about it. She often repeated to me, "You are being romantic. Don't!" without looking at me, and then she would walk away when she saw that I was immersed in listening to pop songs of love.

One day, the two of us were talking about who married whom before my time. She remarked that in the aftermath of WWII, everybody was getting married, and to prove her point, she added, "Even your father married." Soon after her ex-boyfriend "abandoned" her, she met my father, and they were married a few months later. It sounds like she married down and was on the rebound, but their marriage lasted thirty-nine years until my father's death. My father's parents had already lost hope that their son would marry. He was thirty-five.

I was in my mid-teens when I chatted with my mother about a former schoolmate of mine whom I had just seen and had news from. She had told me that her closest friend, a boy, was about to go abroad to pursue his university studies. She added with a loving face that he had asked her, "Will you wait for me?"

My mother exploded into an exhaled laughter as if her lungs had collapsed. She clipped out the phrase, "Will you wait for me?" as one of the notable, rare sayings worth repeating ever so often throughout her life to have a burst of laughter.

I was puzzled by my mother's reaction. I had been naive enough as to repeat to her what my friend had told me sincerely, and I had taken it as something nice. I was left in a quandary as to whether I was girlish or inexperienced or whether my mother was judgmental and insensitive. I kept that in my subconscious, and my consciousness told me to listen to my heart and not to disclose the sweetness that I was feeling.

My friend's boyfriend did come back, and they have been enjoying a long marriage.

Sex was absolutely forbidden to talk about, as we good Catholics know very well. But it was not possible for human nature to be absolutely compliant with the laws and indoctrination of a religious superstructure, no matter how menacing.

In my teens, my mother chose me as the one to whom she could whisper secrets for adults only and with whom she could behave in ways that she would not even do in my father's presence. It was as if I were part of herself, which included farting and jokingly pretending that it escaped her. I was her daughter, and a daughter is special to a mother.

She told me about paternal grandmother's frustration of not being able to "enjoy her husband" because he could be called to work at ungodly hours. She giggled at her being outraged when she learned of the existence of homosexual men. She asked me with boiling curiosity if it was true that our acquaintance's new boyfriend had a big nose, as that is the sign of a big penis.

While on holiday in hotels, my mother would never use the bathtub. When she was young, she heard that a girl had become pregnant by having a bath in a hotel's tub in which sperm had been left. I told her that it must have been a sleazy hotel indeed if rooms and bathrooms were not cleaned properly. But someone else, indeed less gullible and more experienced, remarked that that story was a lie the girl and her mother fabricated to deny sexual intercourse.

While blowing her nose, my mother would lift her leg and press it against her lower abdomen. "Why do you do that?" I asked her. "Because I had two children," she replied. That answer sounded like a giant gong within me, revealing the harm that childbirth marks mothers with. Indeed, she needed to go for a wee often and would announce her impellent need to me by whispering somewhat alarmingly.

My mother was obsessed with smells. She was extremely alert to any smells, which she could detect with her keen nose. I am convinced that her sense of smell was made sharper by her fear and certainty that smells give away the people and environments they emanate from. She wore Guerlain perfume and encouraged me to wear perfume from my early teens on.

She gave me the example of one particular old aunt who used a bidet, that is, washed her private parts, three times a day. She approved of my aunt washing her own panties by hand every day. It was considerate of her not to put her underpants in the general wash. And my mother herself, when she was a teenager, would give her aunt her panties to smell at the end of the day to proudly prove to her that they did not smell at all. I did not know what to do with all those examples of praiseworthy cleanliness of body and soul except to feel a relentless sorrow for my mother's insistence on the same subject, as well as some other formless and nameless effect that I perceived as a dark sort of emotional pain.

When my mother was sixty-one, she broke her knee. Her recovery was fraught with complications, which led to a second hospitalization when she was in great pain. My sister-in-law had to help her walk out of her home by holding her hands and walking backward slowly. She had an internal hemorrhage, and we feared for her life. But eventually, she recovered, and she could go back home. In recounting how much pain she was in that day, she stressed with great pride that she washed her private parts before going to the hospital, no matter what.

All her panties were snow white and looked unused when we found them at her home after she died, so much so that my brother and I donated them, even though we knew the rule that lingerie could be donated only if still sealed in its original package.

When I married, my husband and I went to live in our own home. It was characteristic and had a garden, and we installed a fireplace to make it cozy. When I visited my mother, she would sniff me all over like a bloodhound, with an expression of alarmed anger. It was so unbecoming of her to have a daughter that smelled of firewood.

No matter my inexperience at being a good wife and housewife, it was so humiliating to be greeted by my mother by being sniffed all over, front and back and around. No matter how much she sniffed, she could not stop worrying, and instead be happy to see me and talk about the smell and advise me. No matter how I tried to feel happy in my new life, my cheerfully made choices turned out to be blunders.

## Chapter 9

Spending time at home, in my loneliness, was what I preferred to do. I listened to my own music; I watched my afternoon TV programs. And I dreamed. I dreamed of singing; I dreamed of conducting an orchestra. Many times I turned down invitations to birthday parties with my classmates, making excuses that I had to join my family to go somewhere.

A storm was going on inside me all the time, and I chose to keep it quiet by thinking of music. I started a game with myself: whenever I heard someone saying something, I would think of a song or aria that would follow the words. It worked. It was sort of fun, but above all, turning speech into words in music was a way to make my life lighter. It was like training my mind to obey a pattern, and anxiety was an effective drive to play that game.

What I did not expect was that it would become an addiction. I called it "The Haunting Song," and it took me years to get rid of it.

A real problem was the cause of all my anxiety, but I could not see what that was. I sought help from my mother, who said to me, "Why don't you get a few drops of valium? That way you'll feel relaxed." My brother had just discovered that remedy, and apparently, it worked.

Perhaps the neurologist, a neighbor of ours she had told me to go to, was right. I was sensitive; that's all. But if that was sensitivity, it was excruciating. It never left me. I sensed a permanent stirring that turned into crying when I reached a point of intolerable sorrow. But my crying was never a liberation of excessive pressure, after which people say they feel better, like a blue and sunny sky after a storm. No, crying for me was the top excess pressure spilling over, like milk boiling over, under which the flame was never turned off.

What added to my worry was my father's worsening health. His retirement was traumatic. He found out at his own expense that the boss he believed was his friend was a crook, as all his colleagues knew well. And just before retiring, Dad was targeted with anonymous letters, but he let us know about only one of them, which my mother read to me. It was bullying and insulting, but Dad never reported it.

Dad had shown some signs of withdrawing into himself for some time, but he never spoke about it, as was his character. We were all stunned when a doctor refused to renew his driving license. It was the first red alert that something was seriously wrong with his heart and blood circulation. Eventually, it was decided that he needed surgery, which would be performed in another city. My mother would accompany him and stay with him the whole time.

Before leaving, my father cooked for me all the fish recipes in the big classic cookery book we had at home because he knew that I liked fish better than meat. After two weeks, I was wondering what the matter was with him. I could not stand eating fish every day anymore.

I stayed at home with my brother, cooked for him, and did whatever was necessary to keep the household tidy and running. My brother said to me once, "Do not bother cooking so much for me," in our native dialect. It was his way of thanking me, while hiding behind a screen of distorted words.

The day Dad came back, he could not stop kissing me. He could not believe he was still alive and could see us and his home again.

Dad's weak heart was the reason for my mother to lean on my brother for any kind of support that a woman seeks from the "man of the house." But I sensed some dynamics that were not quite correct. I perceived that she tended to seek advice from my doctor brother rather than from Dad, whom she had known most of her life and knew very well how he would respond to a problem—by smoking more and smoothing the back of his head, without saying much.

Her turning to my brother was a way of raising him from the level of son to the level of chief advisor, including matters that concerned me. The gap between me and him widened, and one side of the gap rose high while my side stayed low.

My ever-smiling, witty mother started nicknaming him "the pontifical arch-physician," which was yet again proof of her learned and refined sense of humor. In fact, whenever I needed medical advice, she would refer me to the pontifical arch-physician, as if it had become a functional title, albeit droll.

\* \* \*

Choosing what to study at university was a matter of discussion in the family but only with the men in the family. By now, I had abandoned the idea of studying archaeology after the terrible experience I had had at high school. I was done with the past and wanted to focus on the future. I came up with ideas that I would like after discarding all scientific subjects, but my father kept saying no. He wanted me to study law, like all his cousins and ancestors before us, but I did not like that at all. It was so boring. True, it offered a lot of diverse possibilities of employment. My brother was more convincing, with his attitude, insistence, and nonverbal language that showed how stubborn I was being for resisting what I was told to do.

So I took up law. Another reason my father said no to all other options of mine was that he would never have allowed me to go to another city to study, allegedly because there was not enough money to support me. But after a few months of attending lessons and reading law books, I quit law. Dad smoked faster than usual when I told him that I could not go on.

I proposed to my father that I could pass directly from the Faculty of Law to some other faculty, but he said that instead, he would "gift" me with a few months' inactivity. That was a great time for me, during which I bought books, listened to cultural programs on the radio, and enjoyed my time both at home and with friends.

Slowly, I developed an interest in another course of studies; a choice that I had discarded before, along with all sorts of scientific studies. I wanted to take up languages at the local university's Interpreters' School. However, I would have to pass the entrance exam first. I reviewed my English diligently by seriously studying the grammar book I had used in high school, and Dad even sent me to Britain for a few weeks to improve further.

I passed the entrance exam, and it was not a big deal for me. But when I told my parents the news, my father held my face with both hands and tears in his eyes, and my mother eyed me as if life would finally be different from then on.

Dad had always insisted on the importance of speaking foreign languages. He knew that they were very important for rounding one's competence in any job. To encourage me even further in my studies, he gave me a fine radio as a Christmas present to help me in my listening practice and to expand my vocabulary.

But I am a contemplative spirit, which is another term for dreamer. I listened to late-evening programs broadcast from faraway countries that I fantasized about. Those were countries that were closed to foreigners and had become ill-famed but also mysterious, such as China and the Soviet Union. The farther the broadcasting station, the more fascinated I was that I could pick up their signal. I was traveling with my spirit to faraway places that I was sure I would never visit.

I realized that I had gotten top marks in English, and I did well at translation at school. I had never thought that it would have been helpful and useful to see which subjects I was good at for the purpose of selecting a higher course of studies. It was life itself that took me back onto the path of my destiny, after a short detour.

The choice of my second language fell to Spanish or German. Spanish was great fun, but German was useful, so I dropped fun and forced myself to study seriously for some useful purpose. My father paid for my studies abroad, which consisted of spending a few weeks in some school for foreigners. My brother was jealous that Dad sponsored me, but never gave him any money for his trips abroad, and he spoke words of doom for what I would find abroad. I suffered from his attitude that reinforced the fact that we were not close. We could have fun playing and singing together, but when it came to serious matters that were not health-related, I knew all too well that I could not rely on him as an alternative to our parents.

The German teachers were exactly what I did not need either. They were all odd characters that did their best to discourage students for the purpose of destroying competition. I could not take their attitudes, and I had never particularly liked German, the useful language. I dropped German and went back to Spanish.

I was accepted by the Spanish teacher like a poor immigrant in her precious country. I did not know why she kept pointing out what I said as if it was a huge mistake, as if anybody—smarter than me—would have immediately found the spot-on term that she corrected me with. She could not stand my Latin American pronunciation, which I had learned from songs. I felt insulted and angered for months. But in the end, she saw I was good and treated me fairly, as she did everybody else.

Many years later, I overheard someone say that Spanish was the easy option at that school of languages, and that any course of studies must offer one easy option. Suddenly, I sensed my body chemistry change for the worse. I felt my blood becoming fizzy all over my body, including my brain, and my energy levels dropped. I needed to prop myself up, as my breath escaped out. I had to force my diaphragm to breathe, and my pulse became faster. That is the somatization following my realization that someone had thought I studied Spanish because it was easy. That's what the Spanish teacher saw and reacted against. She was put out by my falling back. I studied Spanish because I loved it.

The realization that others would think I took the easy option is deeply offensive to me. How could people not see my good intentions, the honesty in what I do?

My vision for my future, as I saw it, was the development of my choice of activities based on enthusiasm. If I feel passionate and enthusiastic about some activity or other, I will discharge it better, improve upon it, become proficient, and offer the world my specialization. There is no failing in that.

The skill and specialization that an expert develops over many years turns into mastery, and mastery is a wonderful carrier of both skill and research, which leads to innovation. When one achieves mastery, that sets an example for the younger generations to follow, be curious about, debate, and contribute to in their own ways.

But somehow, I could not crank up any of my choices and act to expand them. This was true for music and arts and crafts, which were very popular in the 1970s, when I was in my prime. My father did not even consider those activities as hobbies. He could not stand them. I did not have my parents' support or even life's support in the form of some stroke of luck in those directions. So I had to hold back and follow the mainstream like sheep do. Everybody else managed well with that, and I had to show myself that I belonged.

I continued my studies at the Interpreters' School, where I made some very good friends, whom I had lots of fun with. Studying there was a serious matter, simply because it is a school, and we all go to school to learn something that we do not know yet.

At my age, just over twenty, I became aware that it came naturally to me to behave to others in ways that my mother had done to me all my life. It was not so apparent to me when I was younger, but I could see that clearly now that classmates would throw what I said to them back in my face. I felt terrible. I had sworn to myself that I would never say or do things that way, and there I was, behaving instinctively in a way that hurt others, and they reacted immediately. Ah, that's the difference between me and them: I never reacted. I just took it in every single time.

I reviewed my life and saw how I looked down on some classmates who were poorer or simple-minded. I saw my need to know it all before lessons in class and show off. I remembered the time that my mother tut-tutted me for not knowing something I could never have known at my tender age, but thank God, she made an effort to keep on loving me all the same. And now, here I was bursting out to a classmate, "Oh, come on, you don't even know that?!?" He erupted at me, defending his own dignity.

No matter the thrill of studying languages and traveling abroad, no matter the fun I had with classmates who had become friends, the effort that I put in to learn and pass exams, which rested on top of all previous schooling experiences, brought out a characteristic of mine that classmates noticed: I never spoke about school, that is, about the teachers. Absolutely never. How could I? I never spoke of anything that hurt me. I kept it all inside.

My mother trained me well in that. I had nothing to complain about, and if I timidly attempted to express some unhappiness, she would tell me to think of the poor people in faraway countries who suffer from famine and war and to remember that there are millions of people in the world who have been doing far worse than me. I should be grateful and remember that I was lucky. She gave me such advice while walking away to more important business.

If I ever complained to her about the way she treated me, a surge of surprise would not only lift her upper body but would also open all the orifices in her face in a beginning of laughter that stopped at an uneven smile due to the preposterousness of what I had just said. Her words would most often be, "Ooooaaah, what should I say about my own mother, then?" She would then turn her face away from me, as if stirring and joining the dismay of whoever else happened to be present.

Her life had been worse than mine, and I was so cheeky as to show discontent. What I considered my problems were far less important than anybody else's. Even the lady who lived next door told me, from her eighty years' experience of life, "Yours are not the real problems, Anna. The problems of adult life are. You'll see." The poor lady had a husband with Alzheimer's when such a disease was still labeled senile dementia. The only thing that she could do was to deal with him at home. As if that was not enough, they were being anonymously harassed.

What she told me made me worry even more. If I had a permanent cauldron of terrible feelings that kept boiling inside me, what was I to do as an adult? I was pretty sure that I would not be able to tolerate any more pressure, the pressure of the "real" problems.

I had been feeling so intensely wrapped in my own tangle that I was incapable of seeing my mother's humor. I always felt offended by what she remarked about me, but then I dropped to the pits of stupidity when she lifted one eyebrow and plainly said, "But I was joking." *There are so many things that I cannot do already, and on top of that, I do not even have a sense of humor, and that is so bad. Nobody wants a serious friend or wife, or a touchy one.* And yet, I did laugh a lot with my friends, especially when we pulled out some absurdity. We hardly ever laughed at someone. Occasionally, we made fun of a few teachers, but that was to let off some steam.

At the time of my last year at university, with the final exams approaching, my level of tolerance of what my mother would say to me, in her tone of voice and with the charge of her emotional energy, reached danger level. I could not stay at home for long, and I would even take my rest on a bench in the park. What made things worse was that I had to disregard obvious signs of fatigue, which I could not give in to as I was preparing for the final stretch of my studies.

My subconscious compensated for the wuthering stress I felt during the day by sending me dreams of great comfort. I dreamed that I was in a shop full of pastries from floor to ceiling. All the walls and sides of the shop were covered with trays brimming with pastries made with all ingredients available on Earth, including fish. I would eat and eat a wide selection of those pastries that I could pick and choose from, to my heart's content. I would wake up with a sense of emotional fullness that would more or less pull me through the day, and in the evening, I went to bed knowing that I would return to that magical pastry shop for respite and another recharge.

I had to tell my mother about my fantastic dream. "Have you ever thought that you must pay?" she said with half-closed lips, without looking at me while going ahead with her business.

That night I went back to the pastry shop, but I just stood there biting my nails while craving that otherworldly abundance. I did not go back there again. Instead, I began dreaming that I was in a church.

* * *

The years at university were great fun, besides being very demanding as far as studying was concerned. Studying languages entailed a lot of practice, but my mates and I found a fun way of practicing. We would sing many songs, mostly at a bar where lots of students would gather and somebody would play the piano, or at a home where a smaller group of us sang accompanied by a guitar.

I studied seriously during those years. Increasingly seriously, until I was determined to produce a final text for which I would leave no stone unturned. My father laughed seeing me like that. "I have never seen her study so much!" Yeah, it was funny, but I felt a tweak of disappointment. I would have preferred some praise for my diligence, but that is me. I am touchy.

The demands of that particular curriculum, including traveling abroad and making the most of every second for the purpose of improving my languages, were taking a toll on me, which I was discounting. Going out in the evening was great fun, but I began feeling more and more tired.

A former student came back to the university department to say hello to us students and teachers. He had gotten his degree in London, and now he was working in Milan. We were not friends when he studied in our department two years earlier, but we knew each other because the group of students there was small, and we had enjoyed some time off playing cards together. He was well-mannered, professional, and kind. He even rushed to find a chair for me when I arrived one evening at the usual bar where we sang. I had never experienced such kindness from boys before.

We fell in love, madly. It was spring. He was so thoughtful and generous to give me a birthday present—a book by one of his favorite authors. Being on the receiving end of a gift that I had not requested from a boyfriend was a sensation that was new to me and a signal that this person was indeed different and special.

I told the boyfriend I was with at that time—the one whom my mother called "the checkered little boy" and "that stinking boy" because of his jacket and bad breath—that I was in love with someone else. Then I went to see the kind guy to tell him what I had done and that I wanted to be with him. I did not fear his answer, whatever it might be.

Five weeks had gone by since we fell in love, and we decided to marry.

One night I was letting my thoughts run free, waiting to fall asleep in the darkness of my room. A thought was rolling in my head, around and around: *John* is *his name*. That is what Zechariah wrote on a tablet to confirm that his son's name John had been given by God, and it did not just happen to be his wife's choice. I learned that story at the nuns' school. Suddenly, I sat up on my bed with the realization that the John in my thought was my boyfriend. John was destined for me. He was already my husband, even before we had our wedding.

John would call me at home on the phone and visit me when he had a few days off from work. My mother asked me a couple of times if he was visiting to see a certain girlfriend we both knew, and I would reply that no, he was coming here because he was madly in love with me. She never believed me. Perhaps she thought that nobody could love me, or maybe she was putting up defenses against the unsettling realization that her daughter was turning into a woman.

I was preparing for my final exams and practicing extra hours. I was preparing to get married, keeping it absolutely quiet from everybody—first and foremost, my parents and brother. I would call John from a public telephone to make arrangements for my trip to England and our wedding.

The kind of life I had gone through instructed me that I needed to put my mother in front of a *fait accompli* if I wanted to obtain and keep what I wanted. I needed to avoid the painful, chaotic, endless geyser of questions, doubts, worries, and qualms that would hurt and crush me to the point of giving up my love and not marrying anymore, just for the sake of shutting her up and putting an end to the unbearable stress. If I had made the announcement, I knew that my wedding, my marriage, my love would have been treated exactly as any of the things that I had liked before that had ended in failure. I could not allow that to happen this time. I was determined that this was the most important choice in my whole life, and I would not let anyone ruin it.

I passed my final exam with flying colors. Mum was present at the award ceremony, but my dad could not attend because of his health. My classmates and I partied and celebrated all night and into the first light of dawn. A few days later, I left for London, allegedly to have a holiday and see this friend of mine. I had put aside all the money I could to afford the airfare.

I became acquainted with my mother-in-law and my sister-in-law and her husband. I stayed at their homes and was excited and at ease with the British lifestyle. A sensation of stepping into the adventure of the future gave me hope that, at some point, I would be able to drop the baggage of my past that I felt was still heavily trailing behind me.

I wrote a letter to my brother announcing that I would be getting married on such and such a day and added some explanation as to why I had kept quiet. I wrote him hoping to find some understanding that siblings may share. I timed the mailing carefully so he would receive it the day before my wedding.

I called home after the ceremony. My mum answered the phone. I asked her if they had received my letter and she said no. I took a deep breath and said, "Er, I got married." She was very surprised and taken aback but gave me "all her blessings." It is impossible to foresee other people's reactions. Everyone has a different way of reacting to events.

John went to sleep and slept a lot, oblivious to me, who stayed awake and cried for hours. I would find out about my parents'—and indeed other adults'—reaction little by little over time.

I had the law on my side. My mother could not undo what I had done. However, she could not restrain herself from asking me if it wouldn't have been better if I had married one, or any, of my ex-boyfriends.

In my naiveness and impulsiveness, I had thought only of love. In their grounded, parental minds, they thought I married because I was pregnant, and they were not the only ones to think that.

## Chapter 10

Jumping from family life and schooling, including university, into married life and work was a radical change in my life in which I felt a bit lost, as if in uncharted territory. I married the love of my life, and I felt the strong need to have him beside me and walk with me in what I thought were my years of newly found freedom. I was a product of the steelworks of life, but I did not feel ready or prepared to navigate as I thought I was expected to do.

In marrying my husband, I found enthusiasm and a joy in living that prolonged the happy habit of meeting with friends and having fun together that I had during my years at university. In marrying him, I joined an international environment in which I always felt well, as there was enough space around me for my mind and soul to expand and explore.

Ever since the first days of my married life, the thought of death was on my mind as a reminder that my happiness could disappear in an instant. It was not a depressing thought, but it could be regarded as a very odd thought at my age. Millions of people would say that you don't think of death when you're young. Well, I did every day. Perhaps my upbringing led me to think seriously instead of carelessly. But that very thought made me greatly appreciate every moment of living with my husband, while the ever-present warning at the back of my mind reminded me that if it all disappeared, I would indeed be in tatters, but I would not be unprepared for it.

I tasted what it meant to have no fixed working hours. I tasted freedom. I could buy groceries, visit my parents, and just go out and be out at times when I would have been sitting at school wondering what life was like out there. My mother noticed that I had rosy cheeks for the first time in my life. I had always been a pale child, and when I reached my teens, she insisted that I should put rouge on my cheeks. Now I did not need it anymore.

My husband and I were freelancers, and money soon became a problem because of lack of work. It became difficult to make ends meet, and my mother often came to the rescue by imposing on me to take her money, which I often used to pay bills.

My father encouraged my husband to seek employment at the post office. But he soon found employment thanks to my former university teachers, who recruited him to join them, which was exactly appropriate for his degree and natural talents.

Meanwhile, my father absolutely hated that I was wasting my time at home. He was insistent that I should find a job and start working early to ensure that I would build up a pension for my old age. He found an ad that looked suitable for me in the newspaper and told me to apply. It was a prestigious institution, and we all were happy that they hired me. A steady income began to make a difference, and I could even begin to buy some new clothes to wear at work.

We visited my husband's mother and sister in England, where I was happy to feel at home and learn new and different ways of living. I had no difficulty adjusting, and I was eager to get to know my husband's family, both in the present and its history.

My mother-in-law was a singing teacher. What a coincidence! I told her about my singing but did not dare ask her to teach me. One day she tested my voice, and she knew exactly what had happened to it and what I needed. She gave me lessons for free, and for the first time in my life, I was trained to produce my own voice, and I could hear the result—what my own voice really sounded like. My husband hugged me in a proud, loving embrace of me—my true me, the me that had always been there, only paralyzed, and that could now unfurl its potential.

She taught me how to put expression into singing by using an example for me to follow from her own mother, who used to tell her, "I love you, heart, liver, gizzard, and soul." In teaching me that, she expressed how perfectly loved she felt as a child by her mother, who loved her with all of herself. My mother-in-law would say "good morning" to her thirty-year-old son as if it were a joy emanating from her heart to see him every morning. She could be strict too and set clear boundaries, such as forbidding me to be present while she was giving lessons. So I just sat on the steps, listening attentively.

After one year's marriage, we decided that it would be nice to go to the US, where some relatives of my husband's lived. It was time that he introduced me to his aunt and cousins. My mother-in-law gave us a generous gift of money so that we could spend it on our trip. I was grateful and excited to be going to North America to tour it and find family there, too. We planned to meet my mother-in-law at her sister's home in Seattle. I was worried about the flight, but my mother-in-law reassured me.

As we were leaving for the airport, my mother-in-law stood on the threshold, and with a broad happy smile on her face, she said farewell to us by saying, "Have fun!" I was shocked. It was the first time ever for me that a mother was happy to see her children going on a trip. That was the exact opposite of what I had experienced all my life with my mother who, ever since I was a child, targeted me with an endless throw of worries, don'ts, and be carefuls, often to the point of anger and emotional blackmail if I dared say, "Stop, I get it." I felt a heavy darkness for what I never had and others did—the encouragement to fly off and have fun from a self-assured adult who trusted me and let me feel free.

We had a grand tour of the US and a bit of Mexico for a month. We were traveling with our backpacks, and we were young and adventurous and had to be careful about spending money. However, I found a souvenir in Mexico that I really liked. It was a necklace made of short twigs of black coral, which made it look very modern and suited for my age, unlike the necklaces of black coral beads. I had heard of Mexican black coral and was thrilled to see it in a shop. Besides, it would be a valuable memento of the trip, so I decided that it was a good choice and worth buying.

I was proud to show it to my parents, who had known all my life how passionate I was about Mexico and its archaeological sites. My mother immediately saw that what I called black coral was very different from the red coral of the Mediterranean Sea that she knew well. She was so embarrassed of me boasting about a plastic necklace and believing it to be a coral one that she could not sleep. She went to the best jeweler in town, who knew her well, to learn about Mexican black coral. From what I could understand, he did not say much. But her embarrassment, which reached the point of talking to me with jagged breath, made me stop wearing that necklace in her presence.

No matter what I did or did not do, she always let me know that she knew very well why I was doing or not doing something in particular. Her sharpened eyes and sight penetrated into my quiet, intimate intentions. It was so with the black coral necklace, and when I stopped wearing white gym shoes that gave me the childlike happiness of seeing my feet white until she said they were inappropriate. It was so when I walked, keeping my bum in, in the false hope that she would notice it less. On the contrary, she said I must not be silly and showed me how to walk the way she did when she was young, wearing no panties.

I heard her mentioning spanking and noticing buttocks and injections in magazines, on TV, and in movies with such frequency and preference over other subjects that I came to the conclusion that she was pathological about them. I had never labeled my mother in any way, primarily because she was the one who was always right, with no exceptions. But at that point in my life, I was sure, without a shadow of a doubt, that her obsession was pathological.

That did not spare me from the hurt that she inflicted on my third chakra when her attitude of knowing what was going on inside of me sparked a smart smile and sharp eyes on her face, and she spoke out, "Anna, you hate that pediatrician because she gave you injections. You are fearful of injections!" She would thus dive and turn her finger in my never healed wound that I wanted to keep all to myself, and she exposed me naked again. And again. And again.

By that time, I had already stopped giving her hugs and calling her "Mamma" correctly, which I instead distorted into "Mama."

The energy underlying whatever she chose to say to me and how she said it zipped and bounced like a ricocheting bullet inside my guts. I had to keep my arms pressing my belly down to minimize the anxiety that my guts were bursting with. I could not dismiss her as ridiculous or laughable whenever she stood next to me, slouching with her knees bent, saying, "Look, Anna, you're taller than me!" or when she called me one autumn morning to inform me, "Wrap up warm. It's zero degrees in Helsinki!"

Her questions about me and my life were a cause of great distress. Sometimes, I got shell-shocked by what she said and could not find an answer immediately. Every time, I had to think if it was safe for me to answer her or if I would lose anything by answering. Why was I feeling so invaded? Could I perhaps answer in a particular way that would make me feel less threatened? I reviewed all those possibilities within a fraction of a second, while I could feel my energy levels going down fast.

As if words were not enough, and the way I dressed and the way I walked were not enough, she occasionally snatched some pieces of paper with my handwriting and examined it to see what it revealed about my character. She had read one book on graphology fifty years before and kept examining any handwriting ever since.

I felt totally trapped and monitored by my mother, to the point that I could not watch films of innocent people who were framed and accused of terrible crimes. I knew all too well that there was a whole team of cunning thinkers behind a movie who could contrive a twist to let the framed one escape in a way that would surprise the viewers. However, I knew all too well what it meant to have no way out—none whatever, ever. And I felt ever so stupid for being incapable of finding one.

Those were hellish years in my life. I was besieged with big problems on all fronts. Only music could lift my soul into an expanded space where I could breathe and feel light and bright. But the concern that music had the same effect as dope on me made me turn it down and never use it for many years.

At work, I had a boss who was there only for the money. Someone who had met him elsewhere was very surprised to see him at that post. "What is that fool doing here?" he said.

I was doing everything in the office, including everything that would have been his responsibility to do, but he was incapable and unwilling to do it. I often cried in the office for having a hopeless boss that my colleagues termed "horrendous."

"Anna, why do you do it?" my colleagues asked me. Because when someone sees his signature, they would think, *Does he not have a secretary?*

On the home front, my husband was acting strange. I was very anxious that his behavior in public would cause some embarrassment, and I was always on high alert. At home, he was unpredictable, mostly sluggish and sleepy and stoned, and just did not listen to my telling him and then begging him and then shouting at him to stop behaving like that.

Until he confessed to me that his drinking had become a problem.

There had been some denial on my part about his drinking, but the greatest issue was my total ignorance of the matter. I had lived in a family in which drinking was always a no-no. But in the city where we lived, drinking was a widespread problem, and there was a hospital department where not just rehabilitation, but also long-term psychological support was available. People came to be treated there from all over the country.

I had reached a level of suffering that made me angry and desperate. A friend of mine, three years younger than my mother, was worried about me and begged me to accept her advice to see a doctor she knew well. He did acupuncture. She was sure he could help me and even offered to accompany me to his surgery and introduce me, if that would make me feel more inclined. It sounded like helpful, friendly advice, and my husband and I visited him. On our first visit, he understood what needed to be done. "The husband is ill and can be treated, but we'll treat the wife first," he said, "because the illness is in her soul."

While I was mired in those situations, my mother noticed that I had little whiteheads on my face. One day she came to my home to give me a facial cleansing cream she had bought for me. "I *want* you to use it," she said breathlessly with nervousness, silently slamming her palm on the table. She could not bear the embarrassment of having a daughter with spots on her face.

## PART I: THAT'S LIFE

That was the difference between my mother and my friend, between what they noticed was the matter with me and the kind of help they offered me.

I could never tell my mother about my husband's drinking problem, upon my brother's advice, which I agreed was indeed a wise thing to do. I could never tell her about the support treatment that we were having, and that went on for more than five years.

I needed to be careful and quick at changing subjects if I happened to run into some member of the support group on the street while I was with my mother. She was superciliously bewildered at me greeting someone who could have been her cleaning lady and could not help asking me how I knew that person, to which I would dismissively reply that it was a neighbor.

At the support group, all the sponsees who had joined recently were given a pill every day that would scare them off from drinking, as it would cause a heart attack if mixed with alcohol. But my husband did not take that pill upon my request. I had refused that treatment because I was sure that my husband would go on drinking all the same, even at the cost of killing himself. I did not think that declining that pill was a big deal, but when the support group members noticed it, they joined in a chorus of puzzlement. Why would I refuse something that made them stop worrying and feel safe again? It was the group leader who told them what had been discussed among the doctors at the hospital department: taking that pill would have increased my fear instead of lessening it.

I had never thought of that. I had never taken into consideration that my happiness or unhappiness was a subject matter for decisions taken by a team of experts. I was bewildered and incredulous that my well-being was taken into such serious consideration and that my refusal was accepted because my reason to oppose it was important. It was difficult to accept it, but that meant that what I said counted and that doctors—even doctors—did not want me to be fearful.

It was not just from my mother that I had to hide the fact that my husband and I were attending the support group. I felt shame 360 degrees around me. I was very careful that no one at my husband's work or at my work would know. But then, I met three colleagues at that hospital department, and I know that more joined later on.

The support treatment focused mainly on the issues of the alcohol-dependent sponsees, but ample discussion was given to the issues of the sponsoring family members too. As the years passed, I could not help mentioning my rage against my mother and how I was incapable of dealing with her. I said that I was ashamed of attending the group and having this sort of psychological treatment because "I ended up here, not her." Sometimes I would tell the group about a highlight that had happened between me and her, and in the end, I concluded that if she was just an acquaintance of mine, I would not want to have anything to do with her.

Nobody ever commented. That was a space where everyone could express their issues, and anybody could say something to help and relieve other people's suffering. But I do not ever recall anybody saying anything to relieve me, apart from the group leader, who was a psychologist. It was he who made me aware of the fact that, indeed, I could not tell my mother about "bad" things because she would blow up my anxiety with her own, but I could not tell her about good things either. I could not tell her, "Mum, I'm going to get married."

Meanwhile, things at home had changed. I would return from work and ring the doorbell instead of turning my key in the lock, and my husband would open the door for me, smile, and welcome me home with a hug. That's what I needed. In fact, that was what I had needed all my life—to be welcomed home. To be welcomed into a safe haven where the energy of love and peace would nourish my heart and soul and where someone I love would invite me to join in making our life colorful and meaningful by choosing our next move in togetherness.

I became fondly appreciative of seeing my husband sitting at his desk at home while I was making the house pretty and holding the thought of our car parked near the entrance door at the back of my mind. That picture of family peace was in my happy and grateful heart. I could appreciate its full value as I knew by experience what a gift it was to attain such an ordinary state of things and be able to live in it every day.

## Chapter 11

My inner life had been put aside in those years of intense attention to all that was happening, but that did not mean that it was quiet. In fact, it had been screaming for help and solutions all along. Just as when I was a little child and was watching my family members and feeling different, I was watching the whole city I was living in and feeling different; the only one who was so.

I have always looked ten to fifteen years younger than I am. My small figure, size S, was seen as defective for a woman by the local people, who are all big—not just in height but also often in weight. I felt so bad when one of my neighbors was disappointed to see me as I was "like a little child" in her words.

Wherever I went around that city, everybody would invariably address me as "young lady." No one working in shops kept my face in their memory, even when I was a regular customer, and they helped me as if it were the first time I had been there. It was enough for me to drive thirty kilometers away to go shopping in the nearest city, where everybody addressed me as "Madam" and allowed me to feel normal, though a bit startled.

My young-looking face and my trained disposition made several people who were older than me act paternalistically and assured of their priority over me, both in queues and in life. I had to show with a loud voice and waving that it was my turn in queues, as frequently neither the shop assistant nor the person behind me would notice my presence. And when I had appointments with my hairdresser, she would ask me extremely kindly if she could finish first with the other clients, who all looked and acted like mature ladies, and then keep me waiting and finish with me well past closing time.

For many years, I thought of joining the local association of disabled people because I too was treated differently for the way I looked, not for who I was. But becoming an activist and shouting is not my way.

My young face on my small and young-looking body was not taken seriously by adults. When I spoke and expressed my thoughts, people would look at me. "But how old are you?" I heard them say. And when they heard the answer, they would invariably remark to each other, "She looks like a child!" I heard that ad nauseam, but no one ever thought of that before opening their mouths. They all thought I was lucky to look young.

It was also common that I would not be heard, as if my tone of voice and the way I said things could not be heard or understood by the inhabitants of this city; a city where I had a home that for me was just an address. Even though I had a roof over my head, it was not enough for me to feel the comfort of my own home sweet home.

One evening, I was invited to a formal business dinner, as a guest of the organizing lady. She sat me at the presidential table that had ten people. One of the guests who was sitting at one of the other tables in the dining hall came to say hello and shake hands with all the guests at the presidential table. She started greeting everybody from the person sitting on my left, went all around the table, and finished with the person sitting at my right—as if I wasn't there.

All the years that my husband was co-opted in clubs and appointed to important positions, I was present with him at the formal occasions, but I was not recognized or treated as his wife. Every lady looked and had the bearing and behavior of a mature woman and a mother, whereas I felt and knew that I was still immature as if I had been nipped in the bud and could not evolve into a woman.

Unlike me, my husband's secretary was well known to everybody, and everybody greeted her and talked with her. But there was something about me that made me transparent and unnoticed. I found no comfort in thinking

## PART I: THAT'S LIFE

that I could have had fun with that peculiarity of mine and maybe play impish tricks on people. Being invisible meant that I did not count in their world. No matter how much I would have loved to belong, there was something inside of me whispering that going the extra step to belong was not what my soul really wished to strive for. Delving even deeper, perhaps I needed to recognize that I did not have the hardware to belong, and no matter how much I wanted to, I could never change enough to finally get there. Perhaps I was just longing for them to accept me as I was and make me feel like one of them. But they lived their lives in ways that were dissimilar to the way I see life and living. In fact, from the way I *know* what life and living are.

*What am I doing here? Why am I here?* I felt alone and outposted.

It was time I read my life from a different perspective, from another side.

# PART II: The Other Side

My heart was yearning and searching for respite and happiness. In the beginning of my quest, I was faced with responses that only let me down. But I kept up hope, and I searched elsewhere, far away, until I realized that what I was looking for was within myself, and that it was up to me to find it. I began to dig deep, and kept digging deeper.

## Chapter 12

All of Me needed to discuss who would be the best one of me for the upcoming adventure. It was going to be tricky, so this time more than ever, the choice of which aspect of All of Me would incarnate had to be thought out very carefully. The selection would be based not just on acquired skills but also on the peculiarities of each one of me who would be most suited to take on the planned set of assignments. Finally, one aspect of me was agreed upon, and the rest of All of Me bowed to honor the one. With some pats on the back, and the reliance on continued connection to infinite support from home, the elected one got ready and began to dream.

I found myself standing in a warm, golden, glowing vastity. Perhaps I was waiting or contemplating when an energy inside of me took flight and became a white feathered Pegasus that took on the speed of thought. That speed stretched and curled me up to the point of transforming me into form.

I just remember finding myself in a small, white room and arriving there through the doorway on the left, as the door on the right was blocked. I could touch the floor of that room with my feet at the same time that I could touch its ceiling with my hands. Then some energy bigger than me started rocking the whole room, and I held on to both the ceiling and floor with my hands and feet. The room became dark, but I could see light at the end of what seemed to be a tunnel. And then I remember clearly how full of sorrow I was for having to be born.

It was dawn, just after six o'clock. After being bumped and pushed by

Mother Nature for hours, I assume that I went to sleep by half past six, as that is the time that I have been most tired at to this day.

I came to this Earth one day in spring, under the sign of Aries, the sign of new beginnings. I saw the earthly light while the sun was journeying on the last grades of the sign—the power grades of accomplishment of an important mission.

Hovering in the room, I could see my parents' souls exchanging a sense of harmony, gratitude, and tranquility at this momentous experience. A pearly-white lotus flower in full bloom, as vibrant as fire, was spreading its countless petals open flat, covering my mother's groin entirely.

They were very different from my cosmic parents. My cosmic parents were dressed in magnificent embroidered royal blue robes that had shoulder tips curving upward. We were standing together at the edge of a large cave, looking out to the cosmic depth of a night blue sky that was arching in front and below us.

They unfurled a wide scroll, and a long carpet unrolled before me toward the blue infinity. I felt their hands prodding me to walk on it. I admired its beautiful colors and patterns and felt the comfortable wool fleece under my feet. Then the carpet became dotted with small protruding rocks rising from its surface, which became more and more numerous as well as taller and taller until it was rather difficult for me to keep my balance and endure the pain in my feet.

But in that difficult moment, my soul realized that comfort cannot, in fact, must not last forever, as it would keep you small. Rising, becoming tall, gives you a different vision of things, a different view of events, and a wider vista.

But why do I have to suffer? Why do I need to risk falling and hurting myself badly on the rocks while striving to keep my balance? And why is the idea of falling painful, as painful as standing on those narrow rocks?

Why is all of this necessary?

It was my choice.

I responded to the clarion call that resonated throughout the universes,

## PART II: THE OTHER SIDE

as a new grand project was proposed—the creation of a new world, where special laws would be in place.

We were gathered in a large hall. I was dressed in a white robe, like everybody else, and had flowing golden hair. We were all looking toward a raised stage where a male light-being explained to us that we were there to choose our assignments among the ones proposed. He was an ageless being with a peaceful presence. His beard and embroidered robe were signs of his role as a priest discharging sacred duties.

All along the stage and behind the officiating light-being, there were statues of human figures, sitting in a hieratic posture much like Egyptian pharaohs, each statue carrying on its head a square bowl whose edges were gently rounded.

My turn came. The officiating light-being turned toward us with a peaceful smile and wise eyes. He looked at me but did not need to finish pointing at me. I had already chosen. I said, "I choose suffering." He bowed to me and turned to write the symbol of suffering on the vessel of the statue that was appointed to me.

I turned to one side and said to the light-being next to me, "I do not know what suffering is. Let's try!"

But there was an add-on to that choice of suffering that came after experiencing a certain number of lifetimes. I would suffer, but nobody would notice the cause of my suffering, not even myself. I would hide the suffering inside me, while others would think everything around me was fine and that I was fortunate.

My heart carries the very symbols that were engraved on the vessel.

\* \* \*

There had been much talking and discussing in the Heavens to prepare and carefully plan for the earthly times we are now living. Many variables were taken into consideration to ensure that the outcome of the Ultimate Purpose would be honored. Whatever had to happen before then needed to be adjusted in view of the accomplishments of the earthlings and of all the starseeds who came from distant universes to offer their help and share in this exciting venture.

It was agreed that a dispensation be issued regarding the Law of Cause and Effect, whereby souls would not have to work through and learn small lessons anymore. Instead, they would have to work their way back to their true Divine essence by learning big, important lessons and transmuting the heavy energies that they had miscreated through their free will over the eons.

All my contracts were agreed upon by me and by each of the other beings who I had unfinished business with. The outline of my life was sketched. Everything was set and I was ready. An angel touched me where my nose and upper lip joined, and the veil of forgetfulness clouded my mind.

Game on.

But I did not remember that it was a game, even less so the rules of the game. Repetition was perhaps the way to make me remember, but it only managed to frighten me.

Every night I saw scenes in the darkness of my bedroom, always the same. They were like video clips, owing to their size and proportions within my visual field. A sepia-color view from above, perhaps from a tall building, showed me an entire square covered with people wearing boater hats. I sensed turmoil and upset. Then a woman in her forties walked among them. She was the only figure in color, standing out with her blonde hair and red two-piece suit. She looked like she was from a Northern country and more modern than the rest of the crowd.

Sleep would overcome me, and if dreams came to me, they would only show me a young girl with wavy, blonde hair wearing a red camisole and shorts. Her facial features and slender body very clearly indicated that she was from a Northern country. She had a lovely, small, white hairy dog and looked in its direction without smiling. Her mother was with her too, but her entire figure was never visible. There was just the presence of an adult woman with the girl.

For many years, I dreamed of that girl and only of her. That was my only dream unless my digestion was heavy, in which case I was frightened by green, mechanical, crocodile-like monsters that kept snapping their mouths.

## PART II: THE OTHER SIDE

Other than that, my vision during dream time would be pitch black. I remember that clearly: I was fast asleep, and all I saw was darkness. At least that pitch black did not upset me. It was peaceful, and I was perfectly aware of what was happening, even in a deep sleep state.

Sometimes Dad put me next to him in the center of the master bed, and we would chat and giggle, lying back to back until I fell asleep. I would wake up and find my mother sleeping beside me on my right side. And every night, I would see the same scene, a hologram, just above her and moving toward me.

It was a circle of golden metal on which four figures, about fifteen centimeters tall, stood. The figures were dressed like kings of the late Middle Ages, but they did not wear mantles. As a sign of their power, they wore crowns and held clubs in their right hands. One of them was bigger, as were his crown and club. The circle would move slowly in a clockwise motion, letting the three smaller kings come and go past me. But when the fourth, bigger king reached me, the circle would stop, and the king would bend mechanically and touch me with his club. His grinning face was disquieting.

That vision filled me with fear—fear of not knowing why it happened, of not understanding in the least what it all meant, and of being absolutely alone, with no one supporting me in those moments. I felt anxiety, gasping anxiety, for the inevitable stop and touch, which happened repeatedly and was exacerbated by that king's grin.

It was too much for me to bear, all on my own, at that young age. It appeared many times, too many times, but then one night, it did not anymore.

I did not see any scenes in the dark ever again.

\* \* \*

The move from where I was born to another city with a completely different heritage marked the break between my early childhood and the shaping of myself through stricter rules and growing expectations, not just of me but also of my age.

I became engaged in earthly life as anybody "normal" does and must do. I had already pushed aside the fun activities that no adults would think of, such as watching fast-moving, worm-like shapes against the blue sky or rubbing my eyes with some strength to make geometrical shapes appear to my sight. And what a good laugh I had at pronouncing words and hearing my voice outside me.

Life washed over me like a tsunami, endless and relentless. Faced with the criticism of my parents, grandmother, brother, teachers, and even schoolmates, and indoctrinated by loving and admonishing clergy, I forced myself to be what I was not to conform to other people's expectations and wedge my spot in society.

I began to make myself think logically and form thoughts in my mind that were composed of words that needed to be grammatically correct and make perfect sense. I pushed aside my spontaneous mechanism of thinking that felt like a shapeless mass of energy whose light pulses gave and made sense within a fraction of a second. Adults communicate by speaking, and speaking and writing correctly were paramount, especially in my country where literature and arts were traditionally valued above scientific thought.

I tried to conform and made efforts to win others' approval, all the while suspecting that I was making double the efforts that my friends were. "Fake it till you make it" was a concept I never heard of back then, but that was exactly what I was doing, hoping my feelings would eventually disappear. On the outside, I was going where other sheep were going, while an overpowering jam of negative emotions engulfed me into a state of suffering that I considered gone forever as soon as I had a high moment.

All the while, my soul would soar when listening to music. Music would dispel the toxic fog of any negative emotion, make me smile again, and feel like a bright expanse inside me. The pop songs of the 1960s kept me happy until melancholy took over, and classical music became the waves on which I could ride passionate, romantic emotions of unhappiness.

## Chapter 13

**Trigger Warning:**
**This chapter contains descriptions of sexual violence, which some readers may find distressing.**

After spending one year in Milan as newlyweds, my husband and I decided to go back to Trieste and live there. My father and my husband found a little cottage in a neighboring town that they immediately fell in love with. When I went to see what they had chosen, the energy of that house repelled me, and a firm voice inside of me said clearly, *I don't want to live here.* But I went along with their decision and their enthusiasm. My husband has vision, and I don't. He had restored many houses with his father and could see the potential of that small house.

The way I had spent my life up to that point was of intense suffering that I disregarded in the hope of being rid of it. In order to be happy and hopeful at that point, I needed change. I needed new adventures and travel; I needed the company of friends to feel engaged in the everyday life that was evolving outside of me. But in the intimacy of our home, I became more aware of inner blocks that I could not overcome, which made me feel doubtful of my capabilities as a grown-up person. The inability to reach orgasm, not even with the person who was the love of my life, became the cause of deep frustration, and an increasing anxiety of failing yet again was all I could think of. I saw myself as lower than others. Now I saw with different eyes the twinkling happiness of my schoolmates anticipating their afternoons with their partners, and I understood that they were free—free inside, free to feel life, and naturally capable of enjoying it.

I could not understand why I could not, why I was inherently so different from them. The only cause that I could remember from my past was my prim pride of being religious and church-going, which I flung away with no qualms when I began having sex.

Some dreams stood out, but I could not interpret them. They just frightened me, and that is why I remember them so vividly.

I had my arms around the neck of a tiger that was at my side, and we loved each other. Suddenly, I became aware that I was in a dangerous situation, and I was overcome by acute fear that he would mangle me if I made even the slightest movement to release my arms and get away from him. I knew I had to be extremely careful at any given moment, or I would encounter a terrible end.

In another dream, I was walking inside a large church at the time when the plague killed a large part of the population, and I could see lots of dead bodies lying on the floor. There was a priest who was blessing them. He came to me and lay on top of me, like a lover would, in order to bless me. At that moment, I realized I was lying on the floor because I was one of the dead too.

In my quest for a solution to my problem, I sought help from the experts who were available at that time where I lived. I visited them shrouded in shame for needing help for that reason, often crying in front of them. Only my husband knew that I visited them. In any case, I was hopeful that I could solve my situation quickly, in just a few sessions.

It was not just the time that was not ripe for such treatments. It was not just the city that was too small to offer the level of diversity and quality of treatment. It was not just my nation that only imported and translated the advanced treatments that were developed elsewhere in the world, for which we had to wait and then train some experts. It was also my tangle of life experiences that attracted experts who had indeed obtained university degrees but who were both unable and incapable of giving me what I needed. I realized there and then that no one could ever help me.

## PART II: THE OTHER SIDE

Like many, many times before in my life, I was feeling different, with no hope of help. I was full of shame but waiting for the inspiration to find ways in which I could help myself, by myself, on my own.

Living with my husband, I developed an interest in the paranormal. He was comfortable with the subjects that were considered occult, esoteric, and devilish. Thanks to his presence near me, my fear of the unseen slowly diminished, and I found a new interest in the exploration of the subconscious.

I, who had never been interested in reading literature, became an avid reader of alternative healing methods, body language and somatization, astrology, paranormal phenomena, meditation, and Indian traditions—in general, whatever book on non-mainstream thought I could find at the local public library.

I visited a psychologist who had been recommended by a friend of mine. This therapist was the kind of person who thought she had overcome the problems that her clients came to her to solve. Instead, it was clear to me from her manners and reactions that she was unhealed. However, my friend had never noticed anything of that sort. The direct and regrettable consequence of our sessions was that I began to feel irritation and intolerance toward my mother.

It became increasingly difficult for me to weather the kind of "help" that my mother wanted to give me, which began to feel more and more like an imposition, while I was seeking to be happy in the new kind of life that I had chosen for myself. I would have preferred to be living far away and to be left alone in experimenting with ways to build my own life with my husband, rather than being "helped" by a mother who was there to teach me how to do things the way they had always been done before—the "right way." But she was my mother, so I discounted my own feelings and refrained from reacting for the sake of blood ties.

She was so embarrassed about the house I was living in that she angrily whispered that my grandfather would turn in his grave. She helped me clean my house with a face of squeamishness, encouraging me to do chores because "If you do them, you will find them done." That night, I woke up with convulsions in the middle of the night, throwing off the sheets and blanket.

She kept giving me money, as she would for the rest of her life, as a sign of her kindness and unselfishness, and always with an attitude of imposing it on me. I always accepted everything from her, both what she said and what she gave me. I had to. My husband was working but did not yet have a permanent job and was paid twice a year. I was not working regularly, as I wanted and needed to taste the freedom of just living after so many years of school. But freelance work was not enough, not even to make ends meet. My father could not believe that I, such a good girl, would waste my life at home as a housewife instead of working in an office. This made him smoke at an ever-faster rate.

When a daughter needs help, I think it is only natural that she turns to her parents. But I felt a mixture of embarrassment and a fear of being shamed if I expressed my need to them. I could not find any objectivity in myself and stand my ground because I felt I was at fault. I was the one who left home and had nothing and needed to be given everything. My parents had paid for the renovation of the roof, even if that was their substitute contribution to my wedding, which had been free of charge for them. It was thanks to them that I had a house where I could live privately with my husband. My brother, instead, had saved money over the years he studied at university. My sister-in-law had savings from her job so that they could buy a flat through their own efforts, as well as renovate it completely to their own liking, all before getting married in front of the whole family without any burden on their parents.

But in all this apparent trouble caused by my own impulsiveness, my only obsession was the lack of orgasm.

When I was alone at home, I sat quietly and asked questions. Once I asked, *Why do I have negative feelings toward my mother?* An ugly image appeared of a baby, alive and kicking, albeit whiny, and cruelly deprived of his genitalia. My interpretation of this vision was that my mother birthed me as a girl, while I would have wanted to be born a boy.

But the dream that fire-branded my soul was the one in which I, a four-year-old girl, had a kitten. My mother was there, too, and she said, "Shall we paint its eyes?" I eagerly said yes to my mother's suggestion. So she did, and within a few minutes, I saw that the kitten was dying. I was desperate.

I begged my mother to do something, anything to save it. She looked down at me, and with a disdainful half-smile, she said, "But Anna, it was you who asked me to do that." I looked at my dad who was sitting and smoking beside my mother, seeking some kind of support. With no words, just with his face, he completely agreed with my mother and the soundness of her words.

I cried in that dream as if I were wrung like wet linen. That physical sensation of my vagus nerve being literally wrung returned every time I thought of that dream for years. How could she allow a four-year-old child to make decisions? Why did she not say, "No, it is dangerous," as she would have done if I had wielded a knife? How come she always wins, and I invariably lose, even in dreams?

Learning about the Law of Karma was of little support and consolation. It may be true, then, that I asked my mother to castrate my sexuality—the kitten's eyeballs—and completely forgot about my request. Now I had to live with the consequences of my decision. Harsh as it may seem, I had been trained so well to believe that I was at fault on every occasion that even in such a case, I took responsibility for the way I was feeling and the way my mother was behaving to me and had treated me all along.

However, I also had the recurrent vision of an infinite line of ancestors, with me alone attempting to change things. The ancestors were in a single line, marching robotically so close to one another that there was no space between them, and their marching legs and swinging arms had to move in unison. They had iron bands around their ankles, linked to a long chain that kept them enslaved. They were obviously obeying a program that had blanked their minds and will. I was marching with them at the front, being the latest descendant. But my mind was still functioning, and I thought that there was something wrong, very wrong. I turned around and shouted, "Stop, stop! You don't have to do this, not this way!" But they could not hear me and kept moving on and on. I remained alone in withstanding their combined push and weight against me, as I collected all my might and mind power to stop them and lift the spell they were under. It would take me decades to attain a result and see many of them disappear, one by one.

That is the way I felt for so long: I was the one who had to toil hard to release millions of people from suffering. I saw myself flying in the Universe, dragging a humongous fishnet full of miserable people, mostly children. It was so big and heavy that I could barely move. But their misery was mine, too. I could feel it so clearly within me that I could not conceive of detaching the net and flying high and free.

There must be a way, a way out. It is not possible that the future is as bad as the past. "We were born to suffer," my father would say with resignation. But that is hell. There must be a way to heal—a way to feel better, to feel well. But how could I reach that state if nobody could ever help me?

Some help came in the form of news. I heard of past life regressions and that there was one person in my country who had trained as a facilitator. *Let's see if that works*, I thought. *Maybe I can find the cause of my problems in my past lives.*

I began my quest into my past at a time when I was beginning a new life. My husband had stopped drinking, and we were going to the weekly meetings of the support group regularly. My supervisor at work had left, as his contract had not been renewed, and I was free to take care of my office's business with some independence.

I felt a little happiness inside of me as if I had a renovated inclination to do things, to try new things—in a word, to live. Levels of hope rose, too, as I saw that some help was available and that situations had changed. I even felt less burdened by my mother, and I found it a bit easier to relate to her and be together, the three of us.

But the years of dealing with my husband's alcohol dependency, including keeping it absolutely hidden from my mother; as well as a supervisor at work who had been so obviously placed there because he was not wanted anywhere else; and having to cope with a mother who was behaving with me as was her normal while I had to pretend all along that everything was okay, took a heavy toll on me.

When anything good happened to me or when I saw something good happen to others, my eyes welled up much more than they had in the past and much more often than ever before. Watching an athlete win a competition, applauding an intellectual for being awarded a prize, singing happy birthday, saying hello to someone after a long time, finding myself at a famous place, and many, many more occasions triggered this most embarrassing reaction that I could not stop in any way. No relief came from the insight that I wept because I knew that something so good would never happen to me.

It is a reaction that everybody knows I have, and for sure, they have talked about it behind my back. To this day, I still have it. But at least I am not so embarrassed by it anymore, simply because I know that everybody knows. I never had for myself the understanding and compassion that I would readily have for others if I saw that they were distressed by situations that affected them. With some hindsight, I believe that those hellish years exacerbated a tendency that I previously had only occasionally.

But eventually, energies changed, inside and outside of me. I could finally realize my urge to move away from that small town and cramped house and go to live in a larger home in a quiet neighborhood of the city.

Living in the house in that small town has remained a symbol in my subconscious that sometimes reemerges with dreams about invasion of privacy, with perfect strangers passing through my home and even sitting there as if it were some public place.

In the years we lived there, we had cats, as I was so fond of cats, which I could never have before because of my father's opposition to having pets. "It's bad to grow fond of them," he would say, and then it would be up to him to bury them! The average lifespan of our cats in that house at that location was six months. The neighbors were so jealous of their perfectly manicured vegetable gardens that they would kill all cats that scratched the soil and then still smile at us and even be friends when we exchanged a few words on the street.

My husband and I traveled together, especially at Christmas, to be with his family in England. I also enjoyed accompanying him on his business-related trips around Europe. We asked my mother if she could feed the cats at our home during our absence, which she did several times. Asking her to do us a favor was never a smooth process, though. There was always hesitation on her part, which she never expressed clearly. *But that is her,* I thought yet again. *Besides, she enjoys taking a bus and going out a bit, and she loves cats, too.*

One day we came back from a trip, and as we opened the door, we realized that we were not at our home. My mother had re-upholstered the sofa and bought us all the small kitchen tools that she used in her own kitchen, as well as other items that she noticed were missing from our home that she considered necessary to make living in our house complete and functional. She had not said a word during our phone conversations. She meant to surprise us. I could not even think. I could not even scream. I just kept my fingers at my mouth, screaming as if my lips had been sewn up.

My husband talked on the phone with her. She was elegantly surprised and disappointed that we were not grateful for her making our home nicer. She complained to my brother about our behavior. He said something to her that would have never even remotely grazed my conscious mind: "How dare you, at somebody else's home?"

## Chapter 14

It was the first time for me to embark on an alternative healing practice. I came to it with full openness, without expectations. I did not know what could emerge from me, and I was ready to accept any results.

Facilitating past life regressions is not an easy thing to do or an activity that can be taken lightly. A long training and experience are necessary to become a guide who leads someone responsibly through the manifestations of their subconscious.

The facilitators of past life regressions whom I have known are all souls who have been walking on the path of healing and spiritual advancement. This kind of help is not of a lower quality than what a degree can provide. Spirit overlights the facilitators and guides them to lovingly hold space for their clients. On the side of the clients, it is Spirit that guides them to navigate their subconscious in a purposeful direction to see events that will serve as lessons from which to gain wisdom. It takes a lot of courage on the part of the clients to engage in this kind of spiritual work.

Lifetimes and past lives—and parallel lives—cannot be concepts that are accepted and included in the sciences and humanities whose curricula are offered at universities. I know that hypnotists have encountered cases of past life regressions during sessions, but how those visions have been regarded depends on the attitude and degree of openness of the practitioners and their clients.

Those who are daring enough to keep their minds open to possibilities other than what has been taught and imposed on our minds throughout centuries of manipulation, conditioning, indoctrination, and even terror know very well that there is peace and justice in the idea of returning into bodies for the purpose of learning and liberation. Only when I began believing in reincarnation did my idea of God change from fearful to benevolent.

As in every healing modality, the apparent effectiveness of past life regressions depends not only on the level of spiritual advancement of the healer but also on the preparedness of their client's soul to accept the healing. Healing is not to be regarded like the sudden miracles that the Gospels tell us Jesus performed but as a slow process that happens over time, even though some relief can be sensed immediately. Thus I learned that time is an essential ingredient in the unfolding of life on Earth.

What I learned from those sessions is that I cannot set my mind to attain a certain goal according to my perceived needs. It is Spirit that decides what is best for me to see, according to my true needs. Spirit sees the clutter that must be cleared before tackling a more important, heavier block. That caused a certain dissatisfaction with what I saw and experienced during some of the first sessions.

In the beginning, my mind was interfering in directing what I saw. I was not patient enough to wait for images and sensations to re-emerge from my subconscious. Time and waiting are important and affect the result.

Eventually I stopped having past life regressions because I became aware that they did not give me something truly meaningful for the level of spiritual advancement I had reached. I began to seek another type of spiritual work that would give me a more precise direction to head in, while letting me be free and independent to work with my inner realms.

I do not hear of past life regressions so often anymore. There has been an expanding awareness—perhaps Spirit-led—that it is not necessary to see and relive events in order to let them go from the personality.

There is always a lesson to be learned from a vision of a past life, as there is always a purpose in seeing what you see. In fact, what you see may not be a past life. After all, there is no proof of any kind that what appears to your mind's eyes did happen in the past or is happening somewhere else in some universe or will happen in a future that has already happened. A vision may appear, or an allegory, or a view of a world that is not at all earthly. Opening the mind may be unsettling at first, but if fear is replaced with curiosity, the happiness and sense of freedom that ensue are priceless, simply because you are beginning to use the mind for what it really is. The mind is not in the brain of a physical body. You are the mind. It is empowering to learn how to use the mind as the sovereign being that each one of us is.

In any case, what I saw showed me traditions and ways of living everyday life that I had not learned before, from books or historical reenactments, and that were later validated as fairly realistic.

Once a beautiful young vixen appeared to me. She was insecure and did not dare venture into exploring what was outside her den. *Please, Inner Teacher, show me what I am fearful of....*

*Our room is made of wood. Our covered, four-poster bed is a bit off the center of the back wall. On the opposite wall, the entrance door is in the corner of the room. A window on the wall on the right shows the other side of a narrow green valley, at the bottom of which a small river flows. The placement of the bed in the room follows the direction of the river, so that ideally our energy is nurtured by it and flows downstream with it. My father-in-law had this extension built especially for us so that we may live in harmony and happiness.*

*My husband is very handsome. I absolutely love him, and I am very, very happy indeed to be married to him. The energy of our bedroom and of our entire house is conducive to peace and prosperity. When we make love, we are very happy, and I do hope I will get pregnant soon.*

*I am pregnant now, and my heart runs to the future where I see myself helping my son to walk and him growing strong and handsome, like his own father.*

*My name is A Yi, and I am eighteen years old. I live in this green country, but I come from a land where the soil is yellow and rocky. I see my father's home, which is made of animal skins and cloth, and a camel tethered outside. My father is dressed in fur to protect himself from the weather that can be very cold there. There is a woman with red cheeks with him. It gives me so much joy to think of them in that faraway land.*

My husband is the son of a landlord who is strong-willed and commanding. He goes off riding on horseback with his father to oversee the vast land that he will inherit one day. He is so different in character from his father. He is gentle but is forced by circumstances to become a landlord, and that may not be what he would have chosen for himself in life. He must obey his father and feels an obligation as a good son to let his father dominate and teach him.

I try to ease his inner conflict by enticing him to enjoy life and lovemaking with me. That is our way of being together, not by talking and sharing. I am sure things will eventually change for the better, and maybe servants will be happier to be commanded by a gentle lord one day. And there will be descendants, and the family will continue as the lords who will make this land grow in prosperity for many years to come.

The moment of childbirth is near. I am floating in the infinite. I am having magnificent sensations. I sense my baby is coming, and I help his descent by pushing. Everything is going so well, even though I can sense some agitation around me.

The baby is born. He is a boy! Where is my baby? I want to hold him. Let me hold him!

Suddenly, I feel my heart cleft into two, even if my ears have not held what I have just been told.

My husband is dead. He fell off his horse and cracked his head on a stone. I will have no more children.

My pain has blurred the purpose of having a son. That pain has turned me into a woman, a mother, a lady. The happy girl is a distant memory of a time that is no more.

Meanwhile, my son has grown loving, strong, and handsome. Before long, he will be a powerful, respected landlord.

The pain I carry inside of me and the social conveniences of this place and time have forged my attitude into a withdrawn, discrete lady. I could not remarry, nor did I want to. The wound has expanded from a cleft heart into a whole sword that is pointed at the base of my tongue and that keeps my body separated into two halves.

It was only the warm glow of the heart that could melt the blade of the sword

## PART II: THE OTHER SIDE

*and thus dissolve it. The hilt, now free, rises in front of my eyes and, by flipping upside down, shows its true, meaningful shape to me—a uterus with fallopian tubes and ovaries at the ends.*

*Yes, I will have children again, but how will that be possible? I still do not want to embrace anyone anymore.*

*I had to dig deep into my will and into my fears to finally unwrap a cocoon that I had woven all around myself. I dug my heels deep, too, as I feared that seeing my beloved's face again would extend my pain. But I have waited so long to see him again, so why wait any longer?*

*An old photo appears, one of those small prints from a hundred years ago. And his reincarnated face takes shape in the shadow under his fedora hat. Those cheekbones...that obscure, yet piercing gaze...his haughty bearing....*

*It's you, maternal grandfather. I can finally smile at you again, my love.*

Letting go of attachments may seem very difficult because of the strong emotions woven by those cords. The passing of time is necessary and helpful to make us see that freedom from those cords is eventually more desirable than the shackles of suffering.

My maternal grandfather died from illness at age thirty-three in 1926, when my mother was nearly four years of age. My grandmother fell in love with my grandfather and insisted that she wanted to marry him and only him, even though her mother was opposed, as she suspected that he was too thin to be strong and healthy. They married in the port city where Grandfather was working and where I would be born. She had fled there with her father and sister, following the defeat at Caporetto during WWI and the death of her mother three days later.

My maternal grandmother knew absolutely nothing of what marriage was about. Even when she was pregnant with her first child, she still believed children came out of the belly button. Knowing that he would not be around for long, Grandfather bought a haberdashery shop for her, since she was good at sewing and embroidering, besides having a long experience of shopkeeping, which she acquired growing up at her own family's store.

At home, she always made sure that there was fresh ivy on her husband's portrait as a sign of her faithfulness. She was thirty-one and never remarried because a stepfather would not have loved her children as much as she did. And she would have also had to hand over command to her man and restrain her freedom. Instead, she retained her freedom, including the freedom to spend her own money the way she wanted. My mother slept in the double bed beside her all her youth until she married at age twenty-five.

My maternal grandmother was the eldest of three children. After her, another daughter was born. Following those two disappointments, my great-grandmother ascended on her knees the ten-kilometer road to the most sacred church in the region to beg God to give her a boy. Her prayers were answered. However, it was my grandmother who was the strongest character in her family and the one who had a natural talent to manage her father's shop. She also took good care of her widowed father when he needed help for health reasons.

I guess that the hardship that my maternal grandmother suffered by losing the love of her life so soon made her suspicious of romanticism. I cannot imagine how shocked my grandmother must have felt when Grandfather was diagnosed. But my heart bleeds when I revisit with both of them the last goodbye to his children and the train journey together to the dispensary up on the mountains, across the country, and then their last look into each other's eyes and their last touch. Perhaps a kiss, even on the cheek, was forbidden following doctor's orders.

All her life, my grandmother went out of her way to obliterate the true cause of Grandfather's death and make sure that no direct descendant would ever find out the truth. She kept saying that he had died of pneumonia. In fact, he had tuberculosis. He had not been recruited as a soldier for WWI when he was eligible and apparently healthy.

For some reasons that are unclear to us, she considered tuberculosis a scandal. The stories that she would tell us about him, including what he wrote in his letters from the dispensary, did not quite fit like tiles of a puzzle into the course of pneumonia. But we believed her all the same and dismissed our faint doubts at the back of our minds until my doctor brother found out.

At the end of her life, Grandmother had my sixty-eight-year-old mother read some of those letters—the few that she had not destroyed—and tear them up after reading. I remember only one sentence that my mother reported to me—"Dear little daughter! Have her sew a pretty smock." In that sentence, I felt the condensed love that he had for my mother, the longing he felt for her, the care he had for her upbringing, and the sadness of being denied seeing her grow up.

In her last year, my mother said that she did not remember her father at all. She did not even remember ever reading those letters.

\* \* \*

About two months went by after that vision. I felt freer and happier as I sensed that my energy had changed and was more colorful.

An invitation arrived to visit some friends who lived in another city so as to have a good time together over the weekend. The friend who put us up at his home organized a dinner with a female friend of ours and her partner so that we would finally meet him.

Dinner time approached, and I could hear them coming up the steps. But more than hearing them, I was absolutely overwhelmed by the energy of him—yes, him, unmistakably him!—approaching, relentlessly. I was on my own in the flat, while our host and my husband were at the entrance to greet them. I was bending over, covering my open-wide mouth, slapping my hands on the walls, holding my belly, seeking support on the furniture, and frantically stepping here and there in an attempt to reduce the screaming nervousness that agitated me. What would happen in just a second from now? How does he look, and how would I behave all evening?

"Hello, I am so pleased to meet you, finally!"

He has retained the same measured charm, the same elegant manners that veil and tone down a masculine animus, a commanding presence, an inner knowing of the importance of his role. Indeed, he still has an obscurity within himself that makes him mysterious and attractive.

"And what do you do in life?"

"I am a thoracic surgeon. I perform surgery on all organs in the chest, mainly lungs, except the heart."

Grandfather, your destiny of dying young from lung disease was purposeful, and you learned your lesson well to the point of saving lives.

My agitation needed days to reach a level of calmness. Years later, I also heard that the surgeon had a difficult relationship with his father. Again.

Many years after I had the vision of the Chinese lady, I became interested in Chinese culture. I learned the language, I learned tai chi chuan, qi gong, and feng shui, and I traveled to China several times. Through the practice of tai chi chuan, I learned to keep my back straight and my stomach and bum in, as much as my leg joints allow. In reading texts of feng shui, I realized that the room where the Chinese lady and her handsome lord lived was built strictly following the rules of feng shui.

I would also find out that the Chinese lady's name, A Yi, is not a name but a way to address a young adult female relative, meaning "young aunt." Moreover, the shape of the hilt and guard that I saw matched exactly the shape of a type of old Chinese hilt and guard, with the guard extending out on two sides and curving toward the blade.

## Chapter 15

I remember the light-heartedness and the sense of safety that I experienced in the new house when I would wake up in the middle of the night and hear the roar and whistle of the cargo train echoing in the valley. I would smile with my eyes closed, for that whistle reminded me that I was living in my new home, in a green and quiet neighborhood in the city, and living a different kind of life, much lighter and with renewed hope for the future.

For many months, I felt eager to engage in work and various activities, including cleaning the furniture from the muck and bad energy of the previous house and taking very seriously the weekly attendance at the alcohol-dependency help club as my husband's sponsor.

But then, and I don't know why or how, I began to feel that my breath would not suffice. My legs would stagger, and my guts would signal fear to me at all times, while I felt a whole upside-down Egyptian pyramid in my crown chakra weighing down and piercing my head. I would cry in the morning with fear. I needed to prop myself on the wall when walking. I became overly fearful of making mistakes, of letting people down, and if it happened, I would cry loudly in fear and regret as if begging for the forgiveness that I could never give myself.

My mother imagined that I was fearful of having some sort of serious disease. She kept repeating to me, "You don't have anything," with the attitude of a mother who knew better than her children—always at a distance from me, with eyes that penetrated deeply inside of me and a smile that was meant to be knowing.

She advised me to visit a gynecologist, but since everything was okay there—apart from my lower abdomen being "as hard as a table"—she encouraged me to have a consultation with my brother. I was totally trusting of my family members and open to their help.

I went to the hospital where my brother received me in his surgery without his white coat on. The very first question that my brother asked me was, "So, is this the right marriage?"

*What an odd question,* I thought. If somebody else had asked me, I would have been insulted. But since it was my brother who asked me, I just passed and went on to tell him that I felt I had done an awful lot both at work and for my husband in the past few years, and now it was my turn to get some rest and attention. Then I started crying and told him that I was so upset because I had no orgasms.

He suddenly leaned forward toward me and said, "Do you really think that Mum ever had one?"

No, of course not, but I was dead sure that I was the only one in the world who did not have orgasms, and that's that. At the back of my mind, though, I began reviewing some of the women in the family, whether in the bloodline or related by marriage, and doubts began to arise. But, who knows? They could have had the odd hit, while I knew my own life moment by moment. So again, I concluded that I was the only one in the world for sure. Probably the only one ever.

To make me feel better, he also added that statistics report that a very large percentage of women (I seem to remember 40%) do not reach orgasm. But that piece of extrapolated scientific information only managed to aggravate me. I was an aching soul, seeking comfort and solution. I was not a number, and a problem shared did not cut my problem in half.

Talking casually, he probed my true feelings toward our mother, probably having been nudged by her. I had kept my distance from her and given her the silent treatment in self-defense, as I needed a change in the energy that was surrounding me. I told him honestly that I did not hate her and never had. In fact, I did not need to hate her because it was clear to me that she hated herself so much already. I did not need to add anything to her state of mind, as she was already doing the whole job by herself.

We went on with our friendly conversation, and finally, he prescribed me a test to find out if I had spasmophilia. He had discovered it in several patients who felt much better and happier as a consequence of the specific treatment. The test needed to be performed at the neurology department of the local hospital, where a doctor inserted in my hand a needle that was connected to a beeping piece of equipment and a monitor. I lay down on the bed table and the doctor asked me to hold my breath. He waited and noticed that the equipment read no reaction from me. Then he asked me to breathe heavily and hyperventilate, and after a few seconds, the equipment started beeping and kept on beeping. The result of the test was not just positive, it showed I reacted for a longer time than normally seen. Spasmophilia cannot be cured. It is an inherited, genetic condition. The treatment is taking magnesium regularly, for the rest of my life. In my case, it manifested as anxiety and tremors, sometimes even convulsions when in deep emotional stress.

Every evening I would call upon Archangel Michael to feel his strength. I would immediately feel his presence like a wide pillar of light. Then I would pray, "Archangel Michael, let me sleep in your robe!" And I would go to sleep, cozily wrapped in his protective light.

I did not know what was going on with me. I sought an answer from Thoth Tarot Cards, and I always pulled the same card again and again—Seven of Cups, Debauch. I could not make sense of the terms that it represents—overextending, over-giving, overstretching. *Yes, I do feel emptied out,* I thought, *but I am not doing much because I can't, so I am not overdoing anything. I never have. I have never done enough.*

Two years it lasted. For two years, my levels of energy were so low that I felt that I could collapse and die at any moment from a depletion of energy, hence the fear. The name of a good doctor landed on my path like a leaf brought by the wind, and I recovered my energy thanks to the drops and tablets he prescribed me that were all flower extracts.

Years later, I was still wondering what it was all about. An astrologer friend noticed a quadrupled effect of Saturn, my dominant planet in my birth chart. When it is Saturn that affects you, you feel it big time, but if it affects you with a quadrupled effect due to its placement and interactions, then you will feel pushed to the very edge. That made sense.

In addition, a clairsentient friend told me that my feeling so depleted was my energy signaling to me, "Don't use me this way." That was less clear to me. What way was that? But it was an interesting explanation, and I shelved it for possible future use.

\* \* \*

Having energy again made me feel like I had been resurrected. I began to live again. I could even travel and go places to attend groups of spiritual healing and advancement. Feeling free to travel again seemed like a miracle. In those years of lowest energy levels, I felt insecure all the time to the point of panic attacks, but more so when I was out of my home, and I often wondered if I would ever be able to travel again.

In those groups, all participants could express their own suffering in a space of support and privacy that we knew would not be broken. I felt safe, too, and I placed my heart on my sleeve for everyone to see, with the aim of healing by shedding weight from it. I could express some of the deep irritation that my mother was causing me, thanks to the fundamental exercises that we did for healing family wounds.

One exercise that the group leader introduced to us was a meditation to see our biggest teacher. She first explained that the people who are most challenging in our lives are our greatest teachers, so we learn great lessons thanks to them. As we closed our eyes, we thought of our biggest teachers and let them take the form that they represent in our subconscious. Then we opened our eyes, and we began sharing. That was always my favorite part of being in a group, when the healing of one person helps the healing of other participants.

Everybody shared who their bigger teacher was and what form it took. Some said a tall and mighty person; some said an animal. When my turn came, I shared that my biggest teacher was my mother and that I saw her bigger than the Earth. The whole circle burst into loud laughter, except me. But I totally accepted their reaction to the unexpected and hyperbolic size of the teacher that I carried inside of me.

The group participants noticed attitudes of mine that I did not know I had. They would repeat to me, "Let go of control!" but I could not understand what they meant. Until one day, that same encouragement pushed a button inside of me, and I burst out, "No, I can't! Nobody would like me."

That's what it was all about. Finally, I saw what they saw. They detected that my true personality, my real me, was eclipsed by a persona that was performing all the time. It made perfect sense with how I had behaved all my life—in fact, with how I had to behave to be accepted by adults and society.

It is uncanny that I said, "Nobody would like me" instead of "Nobody would love me." For me, it was never a question of being loved, of seeking that cloud of pastel-pink mellowness extending from another to include me in their light. No, it was approval that I was seeking, and approval means to be just liked, nothing more, with a smile, a look, or nod from a certain distance. That is the approval an average performer nervously hopes for in the split second of silence between the final sound and the thank-you applause of a competent public. I never thought I was so effortlessly exceptional as to fire up a standing ovation, although I did imagine that in my dreams as an opera singer. Effortlessness could not coexist in me as long as I kept busy repressing my true nature that did not have approval.

# Chapter 16

**Trigger Warning:**
**This chapter contains descriptions of sexual violence, which some readers may find distressing.**

Sexual issues popped up during the sharing within that same group, and as a consequence, they also emerged in dreams and visions. The prompt of the group leader about what it is that we fear showed me a vision that transported me to another place and another time, long ago. I sensed I was a poor woman living in a very modest house. Every day, my big, rough husband came back from work and shagged me on the wooden kitchen table without a word. My backbone hurt badly, but his need to let out his sexual urge was all that existed for him.

I hurt in my body and in my heart. One day I escaped and ran far, far away, to a foreign land where nobody knew me. I carried my secret within me, vowing that nobody would ever know about it—that I do not like sex.

I saw the woman dancing lustfully toward men and then withdrawing in the dark night to be alone with her secret.

My heart now melts with compassion for that poor woman who mistook rape for sex. She had not known any other kind of approach in that society in which a muscular display of power was all that was expected from men. That same society also dictated that women must marry or else they starve, and so they must submit to their husbands and bear their children, all for the sake of being "protected." She obviously was the heir of generations of women who had been treated the same way and knew of no terms of comparison while living all their lives within their isolated homes.

The duration of that group of spiritual healing allowed a particular depth of soul searching for some of us who were more determined, more empathic, and obviously, less fearful of looking within. I was determined to heal my sexual issue as my main goal along the path of spiritual healing, while I enjoyed any type of exercise and meditation that would allow me to transform and transmute other energies that burdened me and stood in the way of happiness and freedom. Besides, healing can come through pathways that we do not expect to be particularly useful or effective. This was the case of a prompt from the group leader to go within and see what it is about ourselves that we are most bothered by.

A man appeared to my mind's eyes, dressed in a long robe that had turned old and dirty from having been worn for a long time. He looked like an ancient Greek or Roman man who had just passed his prime. He was standing in front of me, barely moving at all. What annoyed me most was that he was blindfolded.

"Reveal your eyes," I said, for I wanted to get to know him. But he would not move.

"Reveal your eyes!" I commanded, but he would not move.

"Reveal your eyes, or I will!" I shouted.

And since he did not move yet again, I lifted my hand and pulled the blindfold from his eyes. I cringed the moment I saw his face. His eyes had been gouged out. I cried like a fountain at that vision. I was the only one in the group who did not share what I saw.

So that is what bothers me most about me: castration. That is a hell of a clue when exploring sexual issues and ways of healing from them. It emerged again, with an unequivocal symbolic image that reinforces and stresses the validity of the visions of the baby boy without his genitalia and the painting of the kitten's eyeballs. And that was not all. For a long time, I had also been seeing gruesome images of a poor baby girl.

Those were all clear signs, and there were enough of them. I was determined to get to the bottom of this issue, with the help of the group leader, who was a facilitator and a teacher of past life regressions. I prayed and I meditated every day for two months before meeting her to make sure that my subtle bodies would be ready to receive a clear and definitive answer. I aimed to go back to the root core issue that had kept me blocked all my life. But in my ego's eagerness to see clearly what happened, I became oblivious to wisdom and did not ask for "ease and grace."

I lay down, closed my eyes, and entered a meditative state, well-prepared to accept whatever Spirit needed to show me. But instead of seeing images, I began shaking uncontrollably in terror, and I woke up on a sacrificial slab.

## Chapter 17

**Trigger Warning:**
**This chapter contains descriptions of sexual violence, which some readers may find distressing.**

Clawed by intense fear, I could only repeat to myself, "Oh, my God, I'm so scared. I'm so scared...."

I cannot help but shake and struggle to calm down, but I cannot manage it. And yet, that is what is expected of me.

They are standing all around me, staring down at me.... What are they doing?

A knife, a large blade is shown. I am so scared.... Perhaps if I don't watch, it will be less painful. One of them says, "If you are scared, you are stupid." Yes, that is right.

I see that my second chakra is open like a red fruit that was stabbed and cracked open wide. But why? Why??

Fear is a bad thing and not of the warrior. I don't know why I am being so fearful.

I stagger when I walk, holding my hands on my lower abdomen, and I do not understand why my legs cannot support me. I have to stiffen my legs to keep my balance while walking. I am feeling full of anxiety, and my breath is jagged and jittery, but I do not see why I feel so fearful. This is wrong. I am stupid if I am fearful.... No, I refuse to be stupid, but I do not see why I am feeling like this.

But you all...you can't be warriors if you do this to other people! This is *wrong! You don't need to do this to me or anyone! Mark my words, priest: The future will prove me right!*

My body hurts in the second chakra because of the deep wound. I will carry this wound and scar into other lifetimes to prove that this isn't the way to treat others.

Now I am a baby girl in this lifetime, with my mother and paternal grandmother looking down on me. I feel a big wedge weighing heavily on my heart. My mother lays me down to clean me and change my nappies. All my body is full of fear, and so tense, tense with fear.

I sense clearly that all this is wrong, very wrong. My second chakra gets stabbed again.

My mother and grandmother are so tall, when I look at them while I am lying down on the table. This scene reminds me of the sacrificial slab. They were there, too!

My mother and grandmother don't talk from the heart. They just perform their duties. But their attitude has made me fearful of being cleaned and washed. My God, having to endure this! How many times, how many? Mother washes me rough. I can't stand this; my legs jump tight together.

It hurts; I hurt inside. I don't want to touch myself. I'm so lovely, gentle, and delicate. What are you teaching me by treating me this way?

I screamed and cried, while the anxiety was so high that I sat up on the bed and opened my eyes. But when the panting subsided, I lay down and closed my eyes again. And I became a baby again, and I saw an angel bending over me and reminding me with a soft voice, "Come on, you have a mission. Go on, you'll make it."

I slammed my hand down in a gesture of angry determination. *Okay, let's be a warrior. Now is the right time to be a warrior!*

*What a stupid mother I have,* I observed. *It is so difficult to go through all this in the first place, and on top of that, I have to fulfill a mission with such a deep wound. I am very, very sorry that my husband will have to be patient with me.*

*I'll go back to that dark place, on the sacrificial slab, and see this through.*

The darkness of this place is barely colored by lit torches. I see those people

## PART II: THE OTHER SIDE

standing around me. One of them is very richly dressed with an embroidered cape and is wearing jewelry and a headdress with feathers. He is the high priest. He is telling me why it is necessary to perform this sacrifice on me.

But behind those words, those gestures, I sense their true intentions.

It is my heart that you really want! But my heart is too strong for you—you who are incapable of knowing your own heart. So you schemed instead to stab me in my lower abdomen, far from my heart that you crave, but you do not dare to even get near it. You are not warriors! Real warriors are not afraid of strong hearts, whether their own or other people's.

I will show you my heart, like a jaguar would do.

My heart tore up my chest, and the head of a black jaguar, baring his fangs, roared forcefully and proudly.

I am the one who travels through time to lift you all, children, to the status of warriors.

Killing a jaguar and wearing its skin won't make you brave. What you steal from another won't get you anywhere. Shame on you and your generations for scheming this sacrifice! It is wrong!

I will take up my responsibility and my karma and go somewhere else, roaming the forest. A jaguar shares a universal heart and understands hearts.

I honor the jaguar for his beauty and might, and my heart is his twin.

How I cherish the monkey! He has the agility to go from one branch to another, like a true heart goes from one person to another, with no preference.

I admire the might of the eagle. He soars like happiness that takes my heart to the sky to see a clearer, broader view.

You are just ignorant people. You don't have the guts to face your own hearts! What you boast about are just empty words. Go through your fears. Let's see if you dare!

My heart is roaring. It climbs up the tallest trees to see the whole land. It has wings, and can fly!

I am a warrior, but a true warrior does not need to kill. I need no arrows or bows. One has to be a warrior inside first.

A large shaft of golden light streams from above into my heart, fills my depleted, limp body, and lifts me up, while I let my limbs dangle. I am abandoning myself in this golden light of life that permeates every fiber of me and replenishes me with truth. I feel I have triumphed, though my body feels that I have gone through the biggest challenge ever in my earthly experiences.

The energy has now changed, and I find myself in a temple full of lights with shiny walls. I am bestowed a shield and a spear. That is the dream every warrior dreams of. The shield and the spear sink deep in my body, and their essence remains as they pass through my body.

I feel the tension of the scar in my second chakra. The blade of the spear opens the scar again, gently, but I am not afraid. I become aware that something is trapped inside.

I am a warrior, and I am brave. I want to see what is trapped inside.

It has a stick as a handle, a hawk beak on top, and is decorated with small feathers. That beak picked and picked to open my flesh in order to go deep inside me and bury hatred there.

Why did they want to put hatred inside of me? That is a kind of torture that you would subject enemies to so that they do not produce any more warriors. By ruining that part of the body, a man is not a man anymore, he can't have children anymore, and nothing can be done about it. Yet my stupid tribe did that to me. But why?

All I want now is just to get rid of that hatred burning inside of me.

I find myself in a temple with a simple altar and a small fire burning on the floor. I sit beside the fire. Water from underneath is gushing through me and coming down the front of me, making my second chakra transparent. I see that the wound is very deep.

A soft voice tells me that it will take time to heal such a deep wound. All I must do is let the water fill it and cleanse it slowly.

The pain is emerging again. No wonder it feels tense here, in my lower abdomen.

All the pain is being drawn into the wound and poured down with the water that takes it away. "Do not touch yourself," the gentle voice advises. "You have been abused too much. Your wound is much deeper than you can imagine. Let only water heal you. Let it take away all the hurt, even just one molecule at a time."

## PART II: THE OTHER SIDE

*I have been very brave indeed. I've tried and experimented, just to fulfill this mission.*

*I look at the forest from the treetops. Now I know what it means to dominate. I share my heart with all the creatures, the leaves, the river, the water, the sky for showering rain over the land. Dominating means understanding all creatures and holding them all in my heart.*

*The water runs through my whole body as currents of blood, sweat, and tears. Knowledge will come to me, carried within all the other streams. But for now, there is too much tension to clear away.*

*All that tension is trapped around my waistline, diaphragm, loins, and spine. I am a warrior, and I am not ashamed to cry. How can I stand all this, and why?*

*The water pulls all the tension, and the tension is coming out. It hurts, but only at the physical level. I feel a weight on my lower abdomen. No wonder I feel my ovaries crushed sometimes.*

It took me years to work out that they did that to me because they did not want me to have children like me. They wanted my heart because it was the most beautiful and strongest they had ever seen. They picked and picked to bury hatred so that I would lower my frequency, and they could reach and take my heart.

A plethora of information was presented to me that day in the vision of the Indigenous man of pre-Columbian tropical America, whose powerful heart prompted me to name him "Black Jaguar." It took me time to acknowledge that the atmosphere of jealousy and envy—energies that I was born with in this lifetime and felt so densely around me—originated in that lifetime.

I doubted for years that it could have been another lifetime. What matters to me are the feelings—those energies that the soul carries through in between lifetimes and into lifetimes—as well as the origination points of behaviors and attitudes.

What mattered most to me was that I felt that I lived exactly as Black Jaguar in this present lifetime. I immediately recognized the high priest as my pediatrician and the lowly servant who told me, "If you are fearful, you are stupid," as my own mother.

Although I was not wise enough to ask to see the root cause of my issue with ease and grace, the Universe gave me what I asked for because my spirit was finally ready to tackle those old energies. They were dark and heavy, indeed, and caused a series of panic attacks over months.

The story of Black Jaguar mattered a lot to me. I felt for his gigantic suffering, and I told my husband the whole story. He listened to me attentively and, being a passionate reader of witchcraft, he recommended that I do not leave the pick around. "It is a dangerous tool," he said, "and you better hide it where it cannot be found so it won't be used again."

*Good idea,* I thought. So I asked in meditation, "Where can I hide it?" The answer started with a clue: not in the bedroom, not in the bathroom, in a place with lots of air.

Then the answer became clearer and clearer, and I felt more and more resistance, as the tears began flowing, and all my body said, "No, not there!"

The only place where those ignorant souls would never, ever reach was my heart.

\* \* \*

One year later, I went to see my gynecologist to have a checkup. The Universe must have nudged me. The gynecologist was a woman who had been recommended to me as an excellent doctor. As I discovered, she was also a poised person who had the manners and sincere behavior that one would seek in a doctor.

She found no problems but advised me to have an echography because many years had gone by since the last one. She referred me to a doctor who worked at the local children's and maternity hospital. The energy of that hospital sent me out of kilter. But I was blessed to encounter a good, kind doctor, a man in his forties. He did a thorough echography, which took longer than I expected, because he found a very large cyst on my right ovary. "Please, do see your gynecologist again and show her my report," he insisted.

The atmosphere of that hospital, and the apprehension and surprise of finding something so wrong that I must continue visiting doctors, made me feel like staggering—a bit like Black Jaguar, who did not know why he could not stand up strongly.

The size of the cyst was so big that my gynecologist told me that it had to be removed. She also added, "Poor thing, you must have had painful periods." She recommended that I get my surgery as soon as possible and referred me to a good surgeon and his assistant, whom she held in high esteem and who happened to work in a small, private hospital near my home.

However, I had been in good health all along, and I was going to leave for a few weeks for my summer holidays. She agreed that I could enjoy my holidays, but she insisted that I should have surgery as soon as I came back.

And so I did. I booked a room in the hospital and went for the scheduled appointment with the surgeon and his assistant. They were not worried. They saw immediately that the cyst was a dermoid cyst that contained tissues such as skin and hair. They explained to me that this kind of cyst is also called "the unborn twin."

Of course, I told my brother of my wish that Mum would know absolutely nothing of all this. I couldn't have taken her energy to take advantage of my state. Distance and silence were my only temporary respite from her.

I also informed my brother about what all the doctors had said and that I would have my surgery in that particular hospital. He was angry at my choice and fearful that I would not have surgery at the big hospital where he worked. What if the surgeon felt sick during surgery? There would be no one to replace him! But I had already chosen, and despite the downpour of words and attitudes that shouted clearly that I was incapable of choosing right and I was ever so stubborn, I went ahead and sort of enjoyed a few days in a single room overlooking a quiet, green hillside.

I went home after a few days and was off from work for nearly a month. All that time, my mother called me in the evening, and I pretended that everything was business as usual.

I visited my gynecologist again at the end of my convalescence period. She was pleased to see me perfectly well and remarked, "You were never fearful."

Of course, I was not. I knew all along what had been placed into my lower abdomen but could not tell her the whole story. I was even sure of its shape within the cyst, even though I have never seen the video of the surgical procedure.

## Chapter 18

The kind of deep spiritual work I had been doing for a few years helped some uncomfortable feelings I had repressed by denial to emerge in my conscious mind. I became clearly aware that my mother never protected me. In fact, "she has never defended me" was the general description of all the characters that I saw in past life regressions, which I recognized as my mother in this lifetime. It was a description that fit her well and was accompanied by no hard feelings toward her. It was just an observation of her consistent behavior toward me over time. However, what I sensed whenever I thought of that description was sorrow and misery that took on the image of a lead-gray, thick fog surrounding me like a cocoon.

I would keep her at a distance, and keep distance from her from time to time, in an attempt to save myself from her behavior that I lived as if I were keeping my fingers in a power socket. She sensed that she could not have her way any longer as she had when my husband was drinking, though unbeknown to her. Now my husband saw clearly the hurt she was causing me and would stand up to defend me.

I was no longer willing to hide my disappointment when she made me a target of her wit yet again, nor was I going to stand by her when she and my husband were arguing. She angrily told my husband to make sure that I laughed because, in her words, "She *must* laugh!" And when I finally stood by my husband instead of being the rescuer and peacemaker, she felt betrayed by me.

But I did not stop helping her in whatever way she needed. She was my mother, and I was her only daughter. A daughter is a servant to her own mother. So must I be. My brother was a VIP and had a high-ranking job that kept him very, very busy, plus his wife had been seriously ill for years and still was.

I kept visiting Mother at her home and became bothered and saddened by newly acquired behaviors of hers that she showed to me as the latest news, such as washing the meat and the cheese under the open tap before eating, and talking to two little stuffed animals that she bought for herself.

I did not mind at all taking her to the hospital to do tests when some unusual symptoms showed up. I could not help feeling worried, as my husband did, because she had the same symptoms as his mother had that eventually led her to death.

The combination of both my and my husband's change in behavior toward her over the past few months, and her own health, caused a most unexpected event to happen: my brother and sister-in-law invited her for lunch on a Sunday, for the very first time after twenty-five years of their marriage.

*That is an odd event indeed,* I thought, *but at least I do not have to invite her to my place as I have done countless times for as many years.*

One invitation on a Sunday became an invitation every Sunday. My husband and I could only imagine what their conversations were about.

That year, my husband and I enjoyed a fine summer holiday in the French Alps to celebrate our twenty-fifth anniversary. We thought of seeing some friends on our way back home, but the news that Mother was in the hospital had me a bit worried, and we drove straight home. It was the end of August, and I began visiting my mother in the hospital every day in the evening, straight from work. She was hospitalized in the department where my brother was director.

She looked okay to me. She could talk and move and walk perfectly normally. She asked me to do some errands and pay bills and bring her the comforts of home, such as her face creams and lotions. I would readily do everything she asked me to. I typed for her and sent off the letters that she had written to relatives and friends.

## PART II: THE OTHER SIDE

But a difference in her behavior showed up at the end of my visits. She would walk to the lifts with me, stay a couple of meters away, and blow me a kiss with a serious face and eyes. I sensed anger in her. But that only made me smile. I knew I had done nothing to deserve that treatment. I knew that her attitude was a consequence of what had been said during those lunches at my brother's home. My conscience was clear, and I let her be free to see things the way she wanted.

She was in hospital for two months. She sort of enjoyed it, in the company of other female patients her age and receiving the comfort of the attention that nurses provided. I visited her every evening, which upset my husband quite a lot. He asked me, "Anna, why do you do it?" He saw my efforts as undeserved service.

"Because I would like someone to do that for me" was my answer.

It became clear that she needed surgery; however, the emergence of some symptoms and her general state of health made doctors decide to postpone it until they were certain she could endure the procedure. Finally, the surgery was performed, and doctors were pleased with her state of health and the results of all tests.

But her time had come. A few days later, she fell asleep during her lunch, and her slumber just progressed. For days, she could barely open her eyes and move her lips to utter some unrecognizable words. She could still hear and understand what we were saying to her, though. I took days off work and kept her company. I softly sang arias that she had known since she was a child.

When it was clear that she did not have all her faculties nor could she move anymore, I crept my hand under the linen and placed it on her hand to signal to her, "Your daughter is here with you."

Abruptly, she moaned loudly, retracted her hand in a flash, and turned her head the other way. I waited a while in the hope that she would calm down and realize that my touch was a loving touch. She reacted the same way. I smiled at her anger. Let her be. Let her go the way she wishes.

That moan, though, did not have the tone of anger. It had the force of a shouted order—not you!

# JAGUAR HEART

\* \* \*

I was having lunch at home when my brother called me, warning me that Mum's breathing had changed, which meant that she was on her way out. However, he said I could take my time because that process would last hours. But no sooner had a half an hour passed that he called me again, urging me to come quickly because Mum was about to die. My husband and I jumped in the car and drove for the ten minutes that it took to reach the hospital and hurried upstairs to her bedroom.

With his thirty-odd-years' experience in hospitals, my brother was astounded at how fast she had died. We all agreed that she wanted to go before I arrived there.

I am not sure I ever mourned my mother. Yes, I was in a daze for days, but I was very lucid and organized all the things that needed to be done. However, I was not even given the time to mourn her, owing to my brother blasting me like a flamethrower. I had to brace myself and defend myself, all the while justifying him for letting out all his pain for Mother's death.

He told me things that he and our parents had always refrained from telling me to my face, thus making me aware of what they had always thought of me and my husband. They considered my marriage simply as a flirtation of mine and were literally waiting for me to announce our divorce. So, that's what they would have wanted from me—another failure, yet again. Or maybe, they did not want me to marry at all and remain unwanted the rest of my life.

Yet, he also told me that our mother kept giving me gifts to prevent me from getting a separation from my husband. I sensed his jealousy clearly. After all, what's new about it? He was sure that my husband was dishonest, as the intruder into our family that he was.

On top of all that, I made the awful mistake of clearing the silverware from Mother's flat, fearing that it would be stolen from the unsupervised flat after the news of her death spread. My brother had a fit. I had altered her home before he could take photos of it.

I had to take care of all the procedures as a consequence of Mother's death, and every time I informed my brother of what I did or had just done, he would edit and improve upon my suggestions and actions. Then I would go ahead and get what he wanted done.

My mother was very fearful that my brother and I would brawl over the inheritance and repeated many times to us, "Do not fight!" When she was still living in her flat, I had gone with her through the items that I liked, only to find out that they had all been meant and reserved for my brother.

When the time to clear the flat came, my brother ensured a fair splitting of the items between the two of us. I did not understand why it was so important to be fair to that point, including evenly splitting Dad's colored matches.

Among the papers we found were my school reports from the Conservatory, from thirty years before, which I promptly ripped up to erase any memories. Anxiety swelled up in my guts when we found all the doctors' prescriptions dating back to the 1970s. Why did she keep those? Were they cherished memories for her?

One funny thing that happened was that my brother insisted on keeping Grandfather's x-rays that were done in 1957 because "they are photos inside."

The tension that had mounted since Mother's death made me so angry that I did not want memories or mementos. I chose a silver dish that I always liked and accepted some antique pieces that Dad had said were for me. Other than that, I wanted nothing.

My husband went through Mother's bookcase and showed me a book he found there: its title was *It Is Not the Parents' Fault*, which was the translation of Judith Rich Harris's *The Nurture Assumption: Why Children Turn out the Way They Do*. My sister-in-law had given that book to my mother. My husband was deeply offended for me, while I smiled wryly. That was so consistent of them—of them all.

\* \* \*

Sitting in the kitchen, I was sobbing. I felt deeply frustrated and impotent. I could not help pouring my heart out to my cleaning lady, who happened to be there at that hour. I was feeling a prickly, dark fog in my heart through which I could not see a way out. She was feeling for me so deeply. She reached her hands for me, held me, and caressed my head tenderly, with eyes welling up. "No…Anna…" she whispered with the voice of her weeping heart that meant, "Please do not cry.…"

*Oh, what's happening?* I thought, as my eyes opened wider, looking at her. Or perhaps it was my heart that was looking at hers. I felt the prickly, dark fog transmute into a fresh air of love and freedom, and my tears halted and stopped, as did my frustration.

In a moment, I forgot all about what went on before, and like a child, I was attracted to the sincere love that an adult lets out as the only answer to what is happening. In those instants, I experienced the alchemical power of love. A power that transmutes any fear or sorrow, like the glow of a thousand candles popping alight warmly as the only answer to cold, toxic darkness. I felt so blessed to have experienced the alchemical power of love. I connected naturally and effortlessly to love, which means that love is within me and each one of us.

Love flows if the heart is open, and sometimes it takes courage to leave that door open, even by a sliver or a crack in the wood. Yes, it takes courage to feel. And it takes courage and strength to keep on feeling.

## Chapter 19

In those years, a choir formed at the institution next door where I was working, and several staff from other institutions similar to the one I was working at joined too, thus creating a choir of scientific institutions. In a sense, that choir had come to me. I was nudged to sing again; I could sing in a team and listen to my and the other voices mingle and create beautiful sounds. Our choir mistress also enrolled us in concerts, which gave us more motivation to improve our musicianship.

The concerts were all announced in the local newspaper. One concert in particular was reported in the newspaper together with an interview with the choir mistress and me. Now the whole town knew that my secret dream was to become an opera singer.

I told the psychologist, whom I knew from the alcoholics' group, but I did not tell my brother about it. "But of course not, Anna. You must defend yourself in some way or another!" he said to me with unprofessional, unofficial body language and a tone almost of compassion.

*Hey, what is that supposed to mean?* That friend psychologist was young, much younger than me, and his ways in behaving to clients may not yet have been honed by some years' experience.

Did he mean that I was right in keeping my mouth shut to defend myself from their criticism? *No, I can't be right. That's impossible.* I was just dodging the hurt, yet again, because I could not help feeling hurt, even when they were joking, and that is not a good trait of my personality. Nor was it good that I could not help but go ahead all the same and engage in activities that they disapproved of but that I liked, even though I knew I would never become a respected professional in the field. That same psychologist asked me if my parents would have felt less embarrassed if I had studied singing at the Conservatory. *What a daft question*, I thought. *I did study there!*

But he was a good person, and one thing he noticed about me came to me as a pleasant shock—that I am a rebel. I studied music against my parents' will. I married without my parents' blessing. And I could add more items to the list, such as studying languages by listening to Radio Moscow, pursuing a spiritual path, attaining a black belt, and studying Chinese. My mother was extremely fearful of whatever was Chinese, and my father would tell me with wide-open eyes and a raised hand, "Mussolini said, let the sleeping Chinese dragon lie!" But the China that I know is lightyears from the China that they knew of seventy years before, in the 1930s and 1940s.

So that's what a rebel is—someone who does the opposite of what her parents want. All along, I had thought that a rebel is one who shouts back at her parents, slams the door, angrily speaks of them as a burden, and cuts all ties with them. No, no need for that. One is a rebel at heart.

Another big trait of my rebellious nature is the yearning to travel. It is written in my stars at birth, under the sign of Sagittarius. It is not just a pleasure or a need that originates from the Sagittarius itself, either from the beast or from the half-human being. It is a yearning that makes the two beings, united in one, use their combined power and imagination and pull back the bow string and aim so that the arrow may reach all the way to the stars.

Traveling for me did not just mean packing the bags and going. "Abroad" is also reflected in my marrying a foreigner, working for an institution belonging to the United Nations system, and seeing people from all over the world pass by me and speaking a foreign language every day, only a few kilometers from my home.

My yearning for traveling abroad is such that it was difficult for me to decide where I wanted to go, until an insight disclosed to me the perfect kind of destination. I would visit sacred places—places that had been considered sacred and revered as such for centuries or even more, in any country and for any religious rite that has the highest good of all as its ultimate purpose.

A proposal to go to Arkansas reawakened in me some deep-seated energy. I felt I was being tugged back to Arkansas, where a long cord was being coiled on a large wooden roll that a magic hand was spinning. The purpose of the trip was to turn on the Atlantean crystals that are buried deep under that area and reactivate them and subsequently spend two days with a lady who channeled Archangel Michael. I had followed Archangel Michael's monthly messages channeled through her for ten years, and I was eager to finally attend such an event.

I resonated with the call of the trip and found myself with a group of spiritual workers and healers with whom I could connect and talk of spiritual matters. I had a great time and made new friends.

While we were in a National Park in the open air, the group leader and organizer of the event invited any of the participants to say or do whatever they wished. One participant let the Spirits of the land speak through him. Another encouraged us to sing a song that said, "I love you. I thank you." After a while, someone said that the atmosphere would be perfect if we had an eagle fly over us. One participant, who was Native American, picked up a drum and started drumming and chanting rhythmically.

A few seconds after she stopped drumming and chanting, I could feel in my heart that an eagle, far away to my right, had heard her call and was circling and thinking, *Shall I or shall I not?* Suddenly, my heart jumped when the eagle decided to fly our way.

But I did not say a word. I was fearful of making a mistake and proving myself wrong. I did not trust my own sensitivity, even though I could feel what was happening so distinctly. A moment later, the eagle appeared, flying low from my right over our group in a straight line and off to my left.

The last thing we did on that day was a ceremony to offer corn to the Sasquatch people, with words of sincere apologies for the way they have been treated by humans. The whole group gathered at the edge of the ravine and looked in the direction of a plume of fog, which resembled a plume of smoke from a campfire rising from the thick green forest below us. They lovingly talked to the Sasquatch and dropped corn from their hands. They all did this, except for me, because my heart was attracted in another direction, about fifty meters away from the plume of fog, where I could feel another heart and pair of eyes hiding beneath the thick foliage. Someone noticed that I was detached from the group and told me that I was supposed to look where they were looking. "I know," I said, and I joined them. But the energy of that hiding heart was magnetic and turned my head and heart in its direction again.

We did not speak words to each other. We sensed each other's shyness and need to stay hidden and still. I felt its wonderment at what humans were doing and an alertness in case they behaved as they can do. I hope that heart sensed my harmlessness and learned that there are human beings that do respect them.

Toward the end of the whole event, one night, I dreamed of my mother. I was on the doorstep of a shop and realized that the lady who was being served at the counter was my mother. "Mum!" I called. She did not turn. I called her again, but again she would not turn. "Mum," I said, "it's me!" She half-turned and said, "I have never loved you," in a spiteful tone and without looking at me, and off she went.

I felt a deep sense of relief when I woke up, remembering my dream. I thought, *Finally, the truth!* Finally, she has not hidden how she truly feels behind a fictitious character that complied with social convenience and commonplace but that also made me confused.

I told my dream to the group participants who happened to be with me at the breakfast table, and the Native American lady commented without hesitation that my mother's words meant that she did not love herself.

I joined the Native American lady again the following year on a trip to Peru, along with the lady with whom I would have my training in Energy Healing Facilitator in Toronto two years later. It was a trip that would take us to many sacred spots of Peru under the guidance of a renowned local shaman.

I could not help crying profusely at the monuments, the sites, and the knowing that I was finally there in a land that had been my own home and that I still loved so deeply, and of which I had read so much about in books.

## PART II: THE OTHER SIDE

I had some reaction to the altitude, which I mostly felt in my guts, but the thrill and elation of sensing those energies and of being there within a group of twenty healers kept me going and absorbing all the scenery, all the stones, all the greenery, and all the colors and music of the natives as if I were breathing the air of home again.

I was surprised at how easily my Spanish flowed out of my mouth. I could express myself effortlessly.

I knew of every place we were going to, but the scenery, the landscape, the plants were all new to me. My heart was full of happiness mixed with awe at the whole landscape that we crossed to reach our destinations. There were various kinds of environments, from the dry tropical land to the olive-green pastures of the Altiplano, to the green rounded hills that reminded me of the place where I was born. But most of all, I revere the mountains, their solidity, and the mystery they hold and reveal only to those who reach their snowy peaks in reverence.

I took several photos of Apu Ausangate rising above a field of golden barley. That view enchanted me. On our way back to Cusco from Pisac, I looked back and saw the shape of Salcantay, black against the sky at dusk. That view made me fearful, as if the towering Salcantay rose sternly above all other peaks in the range.

I could sense the peace and sacredness of Ollantaytambo, where the area on the side of the hill—that was destroyed by the conquistadors—showed me the perfect sense of "as above, so below." The shapes that had been carved in and built with stone were a representation of the way that humans needed to live to maintain the peace that is found in the Heavens. I bowed to such wise governing of the people.

As we started on our way to Machu Picchu, the Native American lady who had summoned the eagle in Arkansas said that she had received a message for me from the Goddess the night before. I asked her to tell me when we were in Machu Picchu, as I wanted such a sacred message to be received in a sacred place. And so we found ourselves in the middle of a wide green space at Machu Picchu, and she told me that she and I once were sisters. She was fourteen, and I was thirteen. We were chosen to be sacrificed to the gods, and our bodies are still buried up there in the ice.

From one moment to the next, I was in sobs.

Two tourists saw me and were so worried about me that they asked me if I needed something. I could not tell them what I had just been told, but instead, I told them that I usually cry when I see beautiful places, as Machu Picchu is. They were surprised that I, an Italian who sees so many beautiful monuments and works of art in her own country, would be so impressed by the monuments in Peru and concluded that they were honored to have met such a sensitive person. Wow, I never thought that I could be complimented for a trait of mine of which I have been so embarrassed all my life.

The story of the two sisters resonated with me much more than my conscious mind would ever know. The fact that I was in sobs so unexpectedly and suddenly means that there is more of me than I remember. "Up there" for me means on Apu Ausangate, the mountain I could not stop taking pictures of. Ever since, I have been wondering if the world will ever hear that archaeologists have discovered two sisters buried together up there in the ice.

## Chapter 20

I started the following year with the resolution that I would travel to visit all my relatives who lived across my country. I kept that promise to myself. I took the plane and flew to Rome, where I visited my relatives there for the first time. From there, I flew to Palermo, where I returned after too many years to reciprocate the visits of my relatives up North.

The first time I visited our Sicilian relatives, I was seven. I still retain memories of that extraordinary, month-long vacation. One cousin, in particular, attracted my attention. She had a funny shape that I found odd but interesting. My mother half-smiled to me, "She is expecting a baby!" That was the starting point for me to work out how babies came to be. One of the next steps would be to figure out just how a ceremony in church could ensure that babies turned out with their parents' facial features.

This time around, I could sense that I was in an area of my own country that has lived influences from distant peoples from lands across the sea. What a difference from the North where I live, where the exchange between people speaking different languages is so easy, and they are so near that they are neighbors. Not so for the peninsular Center and South, stretching out into the sea for a thousand kilometers, reaching into climate zones that speak of interactions with other continents.

I could see the long, thin shape of Sardinia lying on the sea just before the plane turned to land, a shadow trustfully abandoning itself on the blue water. As I stepped out of the plane, the wind, the swaying palm trees, the volcanic soil, and the air itself stirred all my fibers, and I sensed their essence in my DNA, even though I had never lived there.

It was my wish to see my elderly aunts again and my cousins with their young children whom I had never met, including the little girl who was named after my paternal grandmother. When my cousin happily announced to me that the newborn baby girl was given the same name as my paternal grandmother, I felt a club hitting my stomach, reminding me and warning me of my badness as the only one who did not love her. I felt confused, which transpired into my half-smiling at the news.

I was put up in one of my aunts' homes in the same room where I had been many years before when I enjoyed an unforgettable long summer trip at the end of my first year at university. I liked staying with that aunt in particular. She was a distant cousin of my father's. She was so bright, despite her age, and could still walk easily, although she would not go out, not even to church.

The other aunt—my father's first cousin who never married—was a bit of a surprise to me this time. She was staying in a retirement home, as her home was no longer safe for her because of lots of stone steps both to reach her floor and in between some of the rooms. She had visited us in the North several times, taking the opportunity to travel there on work-related activities, and we knew each other well. I expected to be welcomed by her with the warmth that comes from eagerly seeing someone dear again.

Instead, she was busy getting all she needed from her room at the retirement home to spend the day out with us all. She said hello to me as if I were an acquaintance. After a good while in the car, and finishing all of the organizing and arranging that she needed, she asked me, "So, what's new?" She could not help but shed tears in remembrance of my mother, but she did not give me the warmth and affection I would have thought normal within a family. She was not cold or too busy with contingent affairs as a person of her age might be. Instead, she seemed to be absorbed with the memories of the dear ones who were no longer with her, no matter who was around her.

At home in the evening with my host aunt, we chatted and talked about our relatives. Talking about my paternal grandmother, the one who had

## PART II: THE OTHER SIDE

brought me up since day one, she stopped using words at a certain point and instead chose to speak in nonverbal language, as she did not want to say anything wrong or perhaps even hurt me. "...But she had a disposition..." and she tightened and twisted her lips and muttered, "Mmm..." while her eyes looked at me intensely.

For the first time ever, I learned that my grandmother was notorious in the family for being unpleasant. She was called "that terrible grandmother." I was shocked and dazed. Then, I was not wrong, after all. I realized I was not exaggerating when I told some friends about her and me, and ended up saying, "How could I survive?" shaking all over. Oh boy, it felt so strange to be right! My whole body's chemistry turned fizzy like sparkling water. For the first time, I saw that I had spent my childhood walking through brambles.

My parents thought that what was going on between her and me was sort of normal and that I must make efforts to be good. If it had been okay for Dad to be raised by his mother, then it would be okay for Dad's children to be raised by the same person. Is that so, really?

I did not see my dad shed one tear when Grandmother died or at her funeral. He looked at me and said, "Always be strong in life." And when he could not stand my folk style, a bit retro fad of dressing and hairstyling, he remarked with some grudge, "You look like my mother!"

\* \* \*

My paternal grandfather pursued a career in the public service and became a judge. He married Grandmother, and my father was born nine months after their wedding. Uncle came almost ten years later.

My father's birth was a traumatic one. Grandmother had put on a lot of weight while she was pregnant and was very pleased about it. But when her doctor happened to see her on the street, he was shocked and worried by her condition and told her to put herself in bed immediately. What she had thought was fat was instead swelling, which turned the childbirth into a life-threatening process for both her and her child.

Owing to his occupation, Grandfather moved to Northern Italy, where my father attended schools. When Dad was eighteen, the family moved again to another city, where they remained for the rest of their lives. I saw photos of those times when my father was a teenager, and Grandmother was smiling. My father was swelling with rage as if his whole body were ready to explode had he not kept his mouth tight and his head pressing his throat down.

I never knew how Dad did at school. All I gathered over many years was that he liked studying accountancy, and when he came back from WWII, he did not finish his studies in economics at university. Grandfather had to insist to such a point that he took Dad to the university entrance door so that he would finally take his exam, but Dad escaped out the back door.

I guess he regretted that when he asked for a promotion at work, in the belief that a qualification would have been the passport to a higher post. However, what I have noticed in my life is that advancement within a company is determined by personality, and that competence may be low on the list of prerequisites.

With time, I no longer viewed Dad's failure to achieve a promotion or a career within the organization he worked at for thirty years as the consequence of some lack on his part. It was his personality and choices that prevented him from feeling free and reaching out to create an occupation that would be satisfactory to his soul. He did not like his 9 to 5 office job in the least. He only kept himself tied to safety—a monthly income and pension—as his duty to his family.

He remembered fondly the times during the war when he could ride a motorcycle, but he never bought one because it was not safe, and he might have an accident. He never had a hobby. He was sedentary, just like his mother, and played solitaire or read the newspaper from top to bottom, and he smoked a lot. Fighting in the war, his brother's and cousins' deaths at war, and living with his bereaved parents all their life, took a toll on his heart and blood circulation that deteriorated until he died from it. He had raged inside since he was young and kept that rage repressed by smoking. Who knows? Perhaps he also felt responsible for his brother's death.

It was my father who came up with the idea for his younger brother to enter a military career, which was seen favorably by the whole family as

## PART II: THE OTHER SIDE

a good prospect for his future. He passed all the entrance tests successfully and moved to the military academy in Rome where, after two years' training, proud parents gathered to attend the ceremony of Oath to the Homeland.

When war was declared, Uncle was automatically recruited, while my father, who was beyond the age of recruiting, joined as a volunteer. Grandmother thought that she would see her younger son come back from the war, while she was resigned to losing her elder son. But nobody knows anything about the destiny of anyone, not even one's own.

One day, the mailman rang the doorbell. She opened the door and took the mail for the day. It was a note, sent from the Ministry of War, stating that her younger son had been executed by German troops and detailing the gruesome circumstances whereby there would be no grave for the family to mourn him. He wasn't yet twenty-one years of age.

She dropped, sitting on the marble steps of the block of flats, wailing. Every year on the same date, I would see her drooping with sorrow in her armchair, barely able to say hello to me.

One day, when I was a young teenager, I was walking on the street with my mother when she met a lady, and they stopped to chat a bit. My mother seemed to be barely acquainted with this lady, whom I had never seen before. My mother told her why Grandmother could not stand cleaning ladies. Apparently, many years back, Grandmother shouted at a cleaning girl, who before leaving her position spread pins between the sheets of my grandparents' bed.

I was surprised that my mother would tell such a private story of a curse to someone other than family or close friends. Having had to deal with Grandmother for years, the question that rose in my mind was, *Who started it?*

In addition to that, I understood why Dad so strongly insisted that we always pick up our hair from the floor in hotel bathrooms and throw it into the toilet—so as to prevent cleaning maids from casting spells with them.

I was barely a teenager when my mother secretly whispered to me, looking around herself, that Grandmother did not want to be touched any longer after her son's death, and that Grandfather had slept on the sofa ever since. Someone close also asserted that he could not have possibly stayed true to her.

At different times, I have told two persons about my mother disclosing those facts to me. They were both psychologists, of totally different nationalities and ages, but both asked me the same question: "Why do you think she told you that?" I could not find an answer either time. I was used to that and more, as my mother's normal behavior. But the female psychologist gave me a clue about what she found odd: "A mother is expected to talk about children and grandchildren."

My mother also told me of an episode about Grandmother's mother. "Did you know that Grandmother's mother threw a chair at the doctor?" she said. I was shocked. You must always be polite to doctors. I thought, *What a nutcase Great-Grandmother was and what a bad-mannered shrew!* My mother's expression, lifting one eyebrow, signaled to me that such things were absolutely beneath us.

But over time, I learned the truth. Moments before throwing a chair at the doctor, Great-Grandmother saw her four-year-old girl die. Her sorrow and desperation must have been excruciating, like a nail in a cross.

I cannot help but make a link between my grandmother and her own mother in the combined suffering for the loss of their children. The pain of losing children and the fear of losing them young was passed down in our DNA. There was no shame or exaggerated show of sorrow when she cried loudly on the steps of the block of flats, and all neighbors heard her. She could not even visit my father in the hospital when he had a heart attack.

I tend to believe that the stiffness in her legs was worsened by the shock of losing her son. She somatized the thought that she "could not go on." Grandmother stayed at home and never moved from there except to shop for food. She was the cook at home and, apparently, a very good one, as she was highly praised by my dad and all relatives, near and far. I cannot join the chorus of praise, alas. My memory is etched with her doing the same thing every day—spaghetti and steak—except one day, maybe per season, in which she would serve something good that remained exceptional in our memory because we would have it only on that day and never again for a whole year.

## PART II: THE OTHER SIDE

My grandmother had only one friend, who was also a distant relative, who visited occasionally, and we, as a whole family, would return her visits to us. I never knew what Grandmother was like before the war, whether she laughed or was chatty or had any friends.

Grandmother visited her sisters in her hometown of Palermo only twice in her life since she moved North, over more than forty years. She exchanged letters with them, but they would not visit either. A few nieces visited her occasionally, most notably a grand lady mother of nine, for whom our best dish set and silver cutlery were used to serve Grandmother's special dishes to her and her industrialist husband. Her manner of chewing her food with her mouth open and smacking her tongue was forbidden to me, and I could not understand why she was allowed to do that and I was not.

One day, my father encouraged me to comb my hair. I must have been five, and I could not stay still while he was combing my hair. He was telling me that if I did not comb it, it would stink. With hindsight, I noticed that his own mother, the grandmother I was at home with all day, never took the initiative to play with me, her living doll, for example, playing hairdresser and combing my hair.

My mother changed her way of seeing her mother-in-law late in her life. She saw Grandmother as an odd character, to say the least. She asked me if Grandmother had ever sat me on her lap. "What??" I reacted in shock.

I knew inside of me that I had to visit my relatives down South. I had been nudged to do that in time. The aunt who lived in the retirement home died six months later.

## Chapter 21

I was thrilled and proud to be leaving for Toronto for the first time. I had heard of that city as a destination in the 1960s for emigrants from the area I currently live in, and I felt somewhat honored to finally breathe the atmosphere of this cosmopolitan city.

The friend who lived there was Jinna whom I had met in Arkansas and found again in Peru. I would attend the first-level course of her Energy Healing Facilitator (EHF) technique, as inspired to her by Goddess Quan Yin. Finally, I found myself in a group of people with whom I could connect at the spiritual level that I felt I was. Eventually, I found abroad what I had not found in my own country.

I had always been attracted by the Americas since I was a little child. Traveling for a spiritual purpose was the greatest purpose to be going places I could ever imagine. I had never thought of Canada as a destination for my sort of work but was very happy to be going to my husband's country and my father-in-law's city to get to know its atmosphere. I have loved it ever since.

My friend and her helping angel friend Sylvia took me out and about with them, even on a trip to Niagara Falls. I was in Toronto for more than a week and had time to be with them, and I was thankful that they had time to be with me and take me places.

Among a few things that I could do, my friend proposed to me that I have a reading with some healers she knew. I thought it was a good opportunity to seize, and I chose to see the lady who speaks with angels. Doreen was an energetic Torontonian of Irish descent in her seventies. A large pink rose on a dividing wall between her sitting room and kitchen prompted everyone who went to see her that pink, not red, is the color of Love.

Doreen could not only see and speak with angels—including my guardian angel, of course—but she could also look into my right eye and tell me about my soul and my heart, as well as count how many lifetimes I had had and how many years old my soul was. She had meditated extensively the day before we met to focus on my personality and the history of my soul. She told me many interesting things about myself, some of which I resonated with immediately.

I have one of the biggest hearts she has ever seen and a beautiful, absolutely beautiful soul. I was pleased with that. It meant that I did a good job keeping my integrity and increasing my light frequency. In my personality, I carry cellular memory of my skill and talent for music and musical instruments. I was glad she told me about this trait of mine, which I had known of since a very early age. I am very discerning about where I devote my time and effort, which includes not only my interests but also family and friends. Those who have my friendship are extremely lucky because I am very loyal.

I am an Arcturian, and Arcturians do not have emotions on their celestial body. I am on this planet specifically to learn about emotions. But since it is difficult to learn all the various emotions during most of my lifetimes as a man, that is why I had some lifetimes as a woman, during which I wanted to learn about bonding and nurturing but also betrayal and rejection. However, the problem with us Arcturians learning emotions is that we have issues when people do not measure up to us regarding integrity and attributes of value. Since I am very selective in choosing who is worthy of my honor and respect, what I have missed most in this lifetime is people who could set an example for me, whom I could look up to and learn from.

*So that's what's "wrong" with me when it comes to relationships!*

Apparently, I have an honor for the written word. In my incarnations on Earth, I have had many where I was very much into literature and teaching, whether I taught formally or by example, and I was often ostracized by the illiterate masses because I was part of the elite. That is why I have had a comparatively small number of lifetimes because my lifetimes were not just about survival.

In the year 2000, we finished a five-thousand-year patriarchal society. My lifetimes as a man in those times were very good. Conversely, my lifetimes as a woman were not that good because I was very strong-willed. I hate, absolutely hate, being told what to do. I have to make my own decisions and not let others make decisions for me. When I was a woman in a patriarchal society, I hated it, and I finished that lifetime saying, "Next time, I am going to be a man again."

But now a five-thousand-year matriarchal society has started, and Mother-Father God is sending down more Goddess energy than ever. As I see women becoming more empowered, I am happy because my own soul becomes more empowered, too. Many lifetimes I have waited for this to happen, and that is why I have incarnated in this time in particular.

In other lifetimes I have had on this planet, I was a healer. I am very interested and susceptible to various healing modalities. I am always looking into different ones and wondering if this is what my true calling is. But apparently, none of them is my call this time around.

My true call is where I meld my intellect with my heart. My intellect comes in when I share the knowledge that I have by writing books *(What?!?)*, and the heart comes into the love and compassion I have for women on the planet. My heart tells me to empower women because I agreed to do that.

My wisdom can empower women particularly because I have had experiences as a dominant man. Most of the world as we know it is still very chauvinistic, and I mean to help in dispelling that energy. Therefore, my mission in this lifetime is justice, whether in my community or globally.

At work, I went through stress and strain for having to make it and be respected and acknowledged for what I do. It was a struggle. I worked very hard indeed, but now it's done, and it is over. Now I can do what my heart tells me to do.

Having said that and much more, Doreen was complete with all the information on me she had received from high above. Now I could ask her questions. She told me that I had a question hanging beside me that she could see, but she or the angels were not allowed to give me an answer unless I asked that question explicitly. I was puzzled. I had no question in mind, but she insisted. Well, it was not a question that was on my mind but a thought. A word, even. Perhaps that is what angels want me to utter, whether it has a question mark after it or not.

"The only thing I can think of at this moment is my mother."

"What about her?"

"I know it is impossible not to meet again, but I don't want to meet her again in this way." But what way it was, I could not say. I felt the usual mechanical blankness surrounded by lead-gray fog.

We gave some details to the angels so that they could retrieve the relevant energy, and after listening to them, she reported back to me.

My mother did not give me the nurturing that a mother gives a child. My mother treated me "abominably, to put it nicely." Those were the exact words Doreen heard from the angels.

By now, I no longer felt guilty for not loving my mother. I chose her for the lesson. Of course, I knew that she would not make a good mother, but I wanted to be stronger, so the lesson would be in that sense. Although I felt exterminated by her, in the long run, all that suffering has made me stronger. Apparently, it was a "great lesson for both of us." But I only saw that from my viewpoint, not from hers. She had already been my mother in another lifetime when I was a boy. But in this lifetime, "she was more brutal." Yes, this time around, she had more tools.

Doreen proposed to perform a pagan ceremony to divorce me from my mother, but there was not enough time because I was leaving soon. However, something, anything, had to be done immediately to relieve me of the pain I had endured all my life.

She called in Archangel Michael and asked him that he use his flaming sword to cut the ties between me and my birth mother. I needed to be free of the pain, fear, and abuse that were there from the time I was born. I would have no more emotional grief attached to the experience, and I would have enlightenment as to the discernment that it was not my fault and that there is no guilt involved.

I clearly felt Archangel Michael's sword sear through the cords of attachment three times to sever each one of them. I felt lighter and brighter instantly.

Archangel Michael himself said that you honor a parent when honor is earned, which contradicts what our culture teaches that you must always honor your parents. My mother did not earn my honor, so it is not disrespectful of me not to honor her. She hindered me in this lifetime, and that is not acceptable, and that is why Archangel Michael could cut the ties between us.

It was hard for me to accept the fact that I chose her to be my mother and that I chose her for the lesson. Doreen explained to me that I know in my heart that I have grown to be an empowered woman, despite what she did to me. That was the lesson—despite her, I did well. I paid a price in my emotional life, but that's how Arcturians always pay because they want to learn all the emotions here.

"So you learned rejection, betrayal, absolute abuse," Doreen said with a high pitch on "absolute." "And…" She paused to listen attentively. She could not believe what the angels were telling her. "There was even ridicule, they're telling me??" Yes, humiliation was the leitmotif of my life.

Archangel Michael encouraged me, "Go forth now, the remainder of your lifetime, free of that tie, and know that you are not bound to her anymore. And please, do not feel guilty."

I came out of that session doubtful. It was far too much for me to take in all at once. I needed time to process what she said and see whether some or even all of that resonated with me. *I need to sleep on it,* I told myself, *maybe many a night.*

There was a lot to do for me that week. I was excited about the turn that my spiritual life was taking. But most of all, my soul, my guides, were all making sure that I would accept all information, all the new light shining on me, in due time. They make sure that what we earn and gain is welcomed by our entire system, and we feel the newly found Light as welcome. Granted, sometimes tears are needed to wash away the debris that clogs the pathways of happiness. But it was not time yet, not now.

I was still in denial.

\* \* \*

In the spring of 2009, my aunt told me who the whole family had always considered my paternal grandmother to be. In the autumn of 2009, angels through Doreen let me know how they viewed what my mother did to me, and I trust that they tell only the plain truth. The year 2009 has remained in my annals as The Year of Revelations.

## Chapter 22

Following my return home from Canada, not one day went by without me having a realization, an "aha moment," in which I made a connection between what Doreen had told me and various episodes of my life and traits of my personality. First of all, I understood why I do not feel feminine, and I have always enjoyed more the company of men and what they talk about, apart from politics and soccer.

I understood why I was always told that I am stubborn, even though I have never seen that I am. I just feel held up in a straitjacket if I do not have things my way. I saw a thread coming from high above connecting my love of music over lifetimes and had confirmation that music for me is like oxygen for my soul, not doping as I had thought for several years.

My yearning for an occupation or a form of service that would be satisfying for my heart and soul and fill me with enthusiasm and energy was acknowledged in Heaven. That meant that I could hope to find something of that sort in this lifetime.

Doreen's disbelief in hearing "ridicule" allowed me to see that it was okay to be on the side of right. It dawned on me that the psychologists' odd and unprofessional behavior was their irrepressible expression of siding with me and showing that what I suffered was wrong indeed. But how could they never tell me explicitly that my mother was some sort of item in a manual of psychology? Why did none of them ever speak out? I had to cross the Atlantic to find someone who would speak to me clearly, and she had no degree and, more importantly, no fear. Perhaps I would have suffered less, or for a shorter time, if they had explained the relationship between us.

It was hard to accept that all my life, I did not understand in the least what was going on. My mother then was right to repeat that I was "a bit daft." I could never forgive myself for believing and obeying her.

But hang on, that may not be a matter of stupidity. After all, I suffered, yes, and "too much," but I know that I kept my integrity. I never gossiped. I only talked about her with psychologists, whether one-to-one or at the alcohol dependency group or at the groups of spiritual healing. No one else knows what went on.

Denial can be an ugly beast. However, it may serve its purpose as a defense for some time until you see things from a different standpoint. But it was not the only tool that was functioning in my mind. There was conditioning and programming too. There was fear in many forms and names that activated unfailingly when buttons were pushed and overrode my natural reactions so that I would move into a specific type of behavior. This was characterized by no reaction, no words, submission, an awful lot of frustration and crying, raging in private, and hating myself for being incapable of reacting like everybody else did, whether by shouting back or shrugging it off. I bottled myself up to the point of being implosive—explosive only within myself.

Sometimes, I would even be spelled into some hypnotic state during which I discharged whatever duty was requested of me at work and from which I woke up suddenly as soon as I finished, hating myself for realizing only then that perhaps it was not my duty at all. It happened consistently with one of my supervisors, which is very telling about the interaction between his and my subconscious. I saw that supervisor in one of my past life regressions. While he was my supervisor, I dreamed of my mother every single night except two—and that went on for seven years.

But now things were different at work. Finally, I had a supervisor who was productive and worked in ways that fit the current needs of the institution. My new boss had started working there at the beginning of the year, and a new director was expected to take up office one month after I returned from Toronto.

## PART II: THE OTHER SIDE

Taking care of one new member of staff entails a lot of effort and time to give them guidance and instruction on how things work in the day-to-day business, as well as in the whole calendar year. On top of that, a new director—my boss's boss—took office, and that meant a whole new set of tasks to accomplish, with a view to renewing and keeping up-to-date what our institution could offer to scientists as well as to the general public.

Those were two busy years, during which I gave all the help I could to my new supervisor and the director's office for the purpose of materializing new ideas. It was not a new attitude on my part. I had always done whatever possible, as nothing less was expected from all staff from day one. But I was twenty years older. And despite my renewed enthusiasm for the changes affecting my office, I had developed a certain disillusionment for what I had seen and perceived in the past years. I kept working with commitment but no enthusiasm, dutifully saying yes to all requests and working extra hours when necessary.

I began to feel tired in a different way than I had before. I felt that the air I was breathing was much thinner and that I could not endure exertion, such as climbing steps or, worse still, walking on mountain trails during my holidays. But I kept plowing through, as always, relying solely on my willpower, which always replaced my physical strength to keep me going. I even managed to train for my first-level instructor certificate in tai chi chuan and passed the test in front of a committee of masters. *How cool I am,* I thought. *My parents would not recognize me.*

I visited my homeopathic doctor regularly a few times a year. It was December when I was sitting in his waiting room. He opened the door and, without even saying "good day" to me, he exclaimed, "What is the matter? You are not breathing!" He noticed that my breath was shallow, just for survival.

The following month, I was getting ready to leave for Bolivia, another country I felt so attracted to. But there was something that was dampening my enthusiasm, and I did not quite know what it was. I caught the flu somewhere, somehow, about two weeks before leaving, but there was plenty of time to recover, I thought. It was a strange form of flu, though, with a cough, which I rarely have. In addition, I had a high temperature for longer than which I struggled to push down even by taking pills. But, in fact, it _ up again, and at that point, after more than a week of high temperature, I decided to forfeit my trip to Bolivia even if I lost some money. What is more, I could not eat for several days, as even the smell of food disgusted me. I saw the color of my hands not anymore as natural skin color but as yellow and red. I thought that was an effect of so many days of high temperature on my body and eyesight.

I needed help, so I meditated. Help came with a vision of a blue light-being, whom I felt clearly was Lord Arcturus, sitting and talking to me. I did not hear what he was saying, but I knew that I would download and understand later on. I had a vision of four glass vials, about thirty centimeters long, rounded at both edges and full of blue liquid—the same blue as Lord Arcturus. They were placed on my chest, tidily stacked on what seemed to be a vertical strip of rubber that clamped the vials individually and kept them in a horizontal position.

I asked, "How do I use them?" The reply was that one of the vials flipped up in the air and stuck itself into my nostril. It seemed rather funny, but I did not question it.

When my temperature went up again, my husband had doubts, or should I say an insight. That was a suspicious symptom for him. He had me speak immediately with my brother, even if it was late at night. Having heard my symptoms, my brother told me to go straight to the hospital.

I looked at myself in the mirror before leaving. After ten days of high temperature, hardly any food intake, the disappointment of renouncing my trip to Bolivia, but most of all, the fact that I was not strong enough to get rid of the flu, made me so resentful, ashamed, and angry, that I said to myself, *I look like my grandmother.*

We drove to the A and E room, where I had x-rays that clearly showed signs of bronchopneumonia. I was taken upstairs into the department directed by my brother, where an assistant doctor managed to lower my body temperature within a few hours.

I was in a ward there for a few days, during which doctors performed quite a few tests on me to keep an eye on my lungs. I was caged; I was crying.

## PART II: THE OTHER SIDE

Those tests, needles, drawing blood from arteries in my wrists and groin, made me fearful and anxious. Still, I could not eat and had reactions to food, which prompted doctors to send me for a scan of my tummy. And there it was, the culprit: a stray gallstone in my bile duct that caused obstruction. How is that possible? Three years before, I had surgery to remove my gallbladder, and surgeons had said that I was clear. Obviously, I was not. A tiny grain remained there, and it became larger. I needed surgery again to remove the gallstone but not before my lungs were functioning perfectly again.

After a few days in that ward, my brother announced that he and his team had decided to move me to the department of pulmonary diseases. I was happy about their decision. Since I had a pulmonary infection, I thought it was only appropriate that I be treated there instead of in my brother's department of general medicine.

The reason why I was moved to the other department was that my bronchopneumonia, which is not serious despite its long name, became a severe double mycoplasma pneumonia, which is serious indeed. My husband was advised to prepare himself not to find me there the following day.

Now, what could I do at night when I could not sleep for hours, with an oxygen mask on my face, and tied up to two monitors beeping and flashing? I called upon Mother Mary, and she cradled me in her mantle, wrapping me almost completely. I could sense her presence so distinctly. I called upon the Archangels, calling their names and stopping at the name that gave me the most energy. I could stay in that sort of meditative state for a whole hour, sensing those Divine energies that enfolded me and that my body needed so much.

But during the day, I felt furious rage inside of me. Even though my mother was not the direct object of my rage, I knew that this ailment in my lungs was a disease that had built up since my youth, and that I needed literally to get off my chest. All the sadness that I had kept in, all the pain that I had not spoken out about, all the shocks that I had to gulp down, and the wedge that kept my heart down and depressed were all attractors of that infection that developed to life-threatening levels, for which I needed not just human but also Divine intervention.

I remembered the reaction of the two friends who performed the EHF technique on me when we were learning in Toronto. While they had their hands on my lungs, one could hardly keep her balance and had tears in her eyes, while the other one just stepped back and, with both hands on her heart and closed eyes, whispered, "My God, the sadness!"

My mind was lucid as it had never been before. I wonder if it was the fasting that made my mind so clear. Having such an unusually lucid mind, which allowed me to speak English particularly well—I thought—even while I was ill, also kept me in relatively good spirits. I had fun messaging with friends and my brother. I had to ask him about my condition, as the doctors there do not really speak with patients but only with relatives. He told me that the doctors were happy about my reaction to treatment and that I was doing well. I was not surprised.

Still, I could not understand why I was so tired that I could not wash myself. I had to prop myself along the wall to go to the bathroom, and my body was so stiff that I could not walk normally.

Finally, after thirteen days in hospital, I was discharged. I put on the trousers that I had gone there in, and I had to hold them up or they would have fallen to my ankles. I read the doctors' report, and I had to read it twice to begin to believe their words. "Severe" was repeated several times.

My husband drove me home, where we had lived for seventeen years, and I could not recognize the road uphill or the lane where we lived. The houses were the same, but the energy between my eyes and them was totally different. I got out of the car, and the cat looked at me, lowering himself on all fours as if he were beholding something frightful that needed to be revered.

I cried with the tension of all I had lived that morning. I put myself to bed, and my husband visited, reciting the menu on a tray of food he had especially prepared to suit my tummy condition that would need surgery to remove the gallstone. More tears flowed. "Do I deserve so much?" I asked.

At that point, I knew that my taking care of my mother in hospital was being repaid to me.

"You have come back from the front line," my husband said. Then reality sank in, and I realized it was a miracle that I survived.

## PART II: THE OTHER SIDE

I was on sick leave from work for two full months and shrank two sizes. All the time, the cat sat on the bed with me, at my feet, and left me only the time necessary to relieve himself.

One day I remembered to look at my chest to see if the vials had changed. I saw that they were all empty except one was half-empty. At that moment, I understood that the light-beings gave me that blue liquid to breathe and keep me alive and healthy.

Lord Arcturus connected with me again five years later and said, "I contacted you years ago to keep you in good health so that you would be able to accomplish the mission you had agreed upon."

The inception of my mission is this very book.

But what was the blue liquid that kept me alive? The answer was given to me by a reliable source:

*You all know that when you are ill, you stay in bed, you rest to let your body recoup energies and strength. But what happens is that murky substance is not pushed out of your body. It seems like a logical consequence that if you stop, all substances inside of your body slow down, including bad substances that cause diseases. The Light is the only means to avoid stagnation of diseases within your bodies, as its speed and frequency outrun lower-vibration substances and tissues. That is what was given to you to heal from pneumonia a few years ago. That pushed out other lurking substances that have no place in the Body of Light, whether yours or the Earth's.*

*Now Gaia is a light-being and lives on Light. You live on Light too, and that is going to be the vehicle of speed that will leave traces of old substances behind to be transmuted into a higher state of being. The use of Light is what keeps your bodies in good health while traveling at speeds that were never reached before.*

*Invoke the Light, and it will expand with you all. Increase the Light!*

*This is my word.*

*I Am Archangel Raphael*

## Chapter 23

A few weeks passed, and I recouped my health enough to have surgery to remove the stray gallstone. I went back to my brother's department of general medicine where I was prepared and moved to the theaters' floor for surgery. Then back I went, wheeled upstairs to spend a few days under observation.

The doctor on shift was happy to see the golden color of my vomit. That was a very good sign of a successful surgery and my sure recovery! Cool.

My brother passed by and told me that my sister-in-law was not well enough to come and help me. I said that I understood perfectly, and she must take care of herself in the first place. No worries about me.

My sister-in-law had been treating me like the one who indeed and unfortunately knows it all about hospitals and health issues. Following my mother's outpouring of intimate stories at their Sunday lunches, she had taken on a motherly attitude toward me, which included calling me by the nicknames that my mother alone would use. I felt my energy change at the news that she was incapacitated and could not come and help me. I was in a very good hospital, in a reputable department, in the care of renowned doctors and competent nurses who took care of all their patients in the same way, without preference. I was being taken care of, period. There was no one who would take advantage of my state of health. For the very first time in my life, I could say to myself, *I am free to be ill.*

I did not even have those strange feelings that unfailingly trailed behind my illnesses, like annoying rattling cans tied to a "just married" car. I was not angry at myself for not being well. I was not embarrassed for being ill. I was not "daft" for becoming ill. I was not frightened by the people treating my illness. I could relax and let time pass, let my body recover back to health, trust the health service, and be grateful for its existence.

That was a turning point in my life and my energy. It was one of the gifts of the illness. Another gift was a different way of viewing the energies at play at my workplace, which gave me an advantage, and kept me calm instead of stressed out. I also saw that colleagues cared for me and were sincerely worried about me. That was nice and kind of them.

But another consequence of the whole transformational process I went through would reveal itself in a most unexpected way—and in an uninvited, unwelcome way.

In the following months, while I was at home minding my own business, I could sense my mother's energy approaching me. I was still indignant, but instead of reacting, I chose to do something about it. I was the one who had the upper hand this time and the one who could call the shots, pun intended. Every single time I felt her, I put up my hand to stop her and say, "Let me heal first."

I had no intention whatsoever of speaking with her, nor had I any curiosity at all to know why she came back. And back she came, with an insistence and repetitiveness that was not surprising, considering her personality. With the patience I was forced to develop throughout my life, I kept stretching my arm and putting up my hand to stop her and repeat, "Let me heal first." Again and again.

She came back every few days. I could have felt persecuted by such a haunting, but I did not. I had been accustomed to responding patiently to behaviors that would have deserved a completely different approach and be stopped once and for all. I do have the right to live in peace. But that was not the way I could live my life, and it was not the way I learned to live.

I remembered my husband's words when I was still in the grip of my mother's energy after she died: "It's over. It's over!" But his words did not sink in because I knew it was not over. Fifty years of habits and energies do not disappear with someone's disappearance.

And here she was again.

*Will I ever be free?*

* * *

The following year was exciting. My friend Jinna in Canada organized two events that I would not miss for the world. The first one was the level two training in EHF at her home in May, while the other one was a once-in-a-lifetime ceremony in Hawaii to mark the 12-12-12. It would be an effort physically and financially, but I was determined to attend both events.

In May, I left for Munich, where I would hop onto my connecting flight to Toronto. It was a blessing to spend some time at an airport waiting for my connection because my guts were in turmoil. In fact, the airport seemed too long to walk and find a restroom. I knew that was a somatic sign of some energetic phenomenon that would happen during the training. I somehow could sense that there would be trouble ahead, and my guts screamed with the resistance to touching and facing sore spots in my soul.

But meeting again with friends who shared the same spiritual path with me gave me a lot of happiness. We had a good laugh at that beautiful home on that beautiful spot on Lake Nosbonsing. My Inca sister Linda came to visit one day, and we shared fond memories.

The level two training was both interesting and challenging. The meditations in the curriculum pushed me to face ancestral fears. We were guided to sense the dissolving and transforming of our bodies, just like caterpillars do in order to become butterflies. It was a lesson in letting go and trusting the process, knowing that life continues throughout transformations. I was happy that I overcame that fear. I thought that's what I was so worried about at the Munich airport.

On the third day, we sat in a circle and listened to some teachings. Then it was time to have our mid-morning break.

Some pressure inside me began to build up like a hot air balloon being inflated. It grew and expanded until it reached my throat, and a thought in my mind became so pressing that I knew I had to speak it out. The built-up pressure made my heart race and my breath pant. I could not hold myself anymore. I told the group leader, "I need to share!" and we all sat down. The sensation of such a big, new emotion made me cry and shake, but I enunciated, "I had an abusive mother."

The hot air balloon began to deflate as soon as I finished pronouncing those words. It was an effort for me to utter them, and now I could collapse. What I declared was devoid of any hard feelings. All my body moved in unison to let out a truth that was finally stripped of its thick wrap of denial.

All the participants in the circle felt the huge emotions that swept out of me and encouraged me to say more. At a certain point, though, I stopped talking all of a sudden and angrily turned my head the other way. I sensed my mother standing in front of me, and I did not want to look at her. The group leader could see through her third eye what was going on. She told me my mother was dressed in black because she was sad and wanted me to forgive her. She also asked me if I ever loved my mother and if I would be willing to forgive her now and speak to her directly.

I did not need time to think. *Of course, I would forgive you. Of course, I loved you very, very much indeed.* How could a child not love her own mother, for goodness' sake?

Then my mother's dress turned into colors. She was happy.

I took Archangel Michael's sword and cut the cords of attachment between us. We were detached. However, I was absolutely exhausted and in need of recovering on all four levels: physical, mental, emotional, and spiritual.

Several participants shed tears with me, and some were prompted to share their own traumas.

My need to drop that big toxic cargo changed the agenda for the day. The group leader had us write forgiveness letters that we subsequently burned to release their ashes into the waters of the peaceful lake.

* * *

# PART II: THE OTHER SIDE

Crossing half of the world to reach the middle of the Pacific Ocean and staying there for one week was an endeavor that I was determined and eager to accomplish. However, I had not allowed for the expenditure of my energy on traveling, delays and re-routing, adjusting to twelve time zones, and withstanding predictable spiritual bumps from the various activities in the retreat. I never consider how much energy it costs me to do something—anything. If I see that it is necessary, I just do it.

The problem is, if I do not see the premise, I do not see the consequences either. So at the end of everything I do not understand why I am overtired and in low spirits. Never mind. One day I will learn.

I was elated to take off from LA Airport and have an overwhelming view of the Sierra. I could feel the spine of North America's coastline reaching all the way up North to the land of ice and coming toward me to the flatlands of Los Angeles to spread in a vastness that is unknown in my country. I could sense the Sierra rolling into the blue ocean and cascading below the waters to run wide and unseen paths beyond ever-shifting horizons.

The lady sitting next to me in the window seat could clearly understand from my keen looks that it was my first time ever in Hawaii, and she was so kind as to fully open the window screen and sit back to let me have a full view of the landscape—all lava. How amazing!

I love rocks and minerals. I can sense their energy just by looking at them. I can feel their energy in my hand to the point of vibrating all the way up to my elbow. The participants in the retreat, whom I had already met during the EHF training in Canada, knew about that trait of mine and asked me what the energy of the place felt like. I sensed a "waiting" energy. But I could not explain why it was "waiting." Perhaps I myself had to wait before finding out why.

I was in a group of about twenty women and one man. He was our loyal strong counterbalancing energy in many training sessions and retreats of our group, and a local from Honolulu. Two ladies, both shamans, would take care of the catering for us. They would cook local food, which was inviting, varied, and abundant. What a feast we found on the table when it was time to eat, and we gathered holding hands in a circle to bless the food.

Shortly after I arrived, one of the shaman ladies told me she could do some special kind of massage, if I wanted to try. I said yes, that would be very nice. When we were in her room, she confessed that she did not usually come forward like that to people she had just met, and she herself was surprised at the way she approached me. She also told me that she was Native American and that she carried owl medicine.

"Oh…it's you!"

Then I told her about a dream that I had a few weeks before. I saw a flock of eagles flying together toward the west, and I was one of them. The eagle flying next to me was white. It turned its head toward me, and I realized that it was a barn owl. It kept looking at me intensely with its black eyes as if telling me something deep.

We had reconnected. Our souls had recognized each other.

* * *

The highlight of the retreat was a ceremony at the warm ponds near Hilo to celebrate 12-12-12 at noon. Other than that, the program of the retreat spanned over four days and was varied and included visits to sacred places and some fun extra activities besides the usual activities in class. Two sacred but fun activities were swimming with manta rays on one day and with dolphins on another day. I told the organizer that I was not much of a swimmer, but I would not have missed those awesome opportunities, and I registered for both.

I did not take into account how jet-lagged and tired I was. I just went along with everybody else's enthusiasm. I was the only one coming from twelve time zones away, having been rerouted because of snowstorms and reaching there half a day late. Most of the other participants came from Toronto but had arrived early to organize things at the house and had time to adjust and to do some sightseeing.

Instead, I was picked up at the airport to be taken straight up to Mauna Kea at the altitude of the visitors' center, where we stayed until night to see the stars, both with and without the help of amateur astronomers and their telescopes. What a sight it was to see Orion lying horizontally! The moon, too, was at a different angle than the way I saw it from my home.

The next two days were devoted to in-house retreat activities, and at the end of the second day, we left to reach the dock before sunset, where a boat would take us to where the manta rays gathered at night. The boat ride took us to the other end of the wide bay of Kona. We were not far from the coast where the best houses were located. The water was shallow—maybe three meters deep.

While we were still moving, we were given instructions on how to wear wetsuits and masks with snorkels and what to do and not to do in the water when watching the manta rays. We took a group picture in which I was still smiling.

The sun went down quickly at that latitude, and soon it was dark. My stomach began to feel funny before we reached the place where we anchored. The boat was left to the cradling of the water to allow for an inspection of the waters and make sure that mantas would come there. That took too long for me, as I was already frightened at having to wear a wetsuit and a mask, which made me feel absolutely claustrophobic.

It was my turn to get into the water and reach the floating railing that was about two meters from the boat. I was panting with fear, but somehow I reached the railing. However, I did not go to the spot that I was told to go to. Instead, I held onto the spot nearest to the boat steps. I was told to move farther down the railing, but I think my reaction was so clear that it even surprised me. I said "no" as best I could with the snorkel in my mouth. My neck was stiff, and I was so nervous that my head moved rapidly, albeit imperceptibly, from side to side.

Our guide understood me and what was going on and had me stay where I chose while the other participants swam around me and slid down farther along. Submerged lights went on, and more people gathered where we were, coming both snorkeling and on kayaks.

Then the mantas came. Those little mantas reached where the water was just deep enough for them to dance. That's what they do. They come flying, batting their wings with grace and slowness, caressing the water that caresses them. Attracted by the lights, they sense the call of adventure and exploration and move in perfect freedom across the water at a pace that knows no haste.

What a lesson in light-heartedness I had from one of them. The smallest one chose me to dance with. It cavorted in a circle below me, in slow motion, filling every second of the time passing with utmost wisdom of how to use time and space. Its happiness expressed itself with graceful movements and the emanation of itself all around. It was light-hearted and made me feel its light-heartedness in the middle of my fright.

In its dance, it turned from black to white, trustfully exposing its belly to me and showing its unique constellation of spots on it that, like a signature, revealed its name to me. It was such a show of beauty, grace, happiness, and trust. "Come, dance with me, and feel life move you" was her call to me into its way of being.

But in my way of being, five minutes were quite enough to stay in the water, and I wanted to go back on board. I heard the guide on the boat say to me, "Anna, you are doing awesome," to encourage me, but I knew it was not true. I was doing abysmally.

I went back on board and waited there for an eternity—that is, for the whole thing to finish and for everybody to come back on board—slowly, of course. That was paid-for leisure time, and customers wanted to enjoy it as long as possible, including their hot chocolate to warm up after staying in the water for an hour or more.

The boat just did not stop rolling and pitching, and the waves kept hitting it. I vomited constantly until we reached the dock. My esophagus was so irritated that I feared I would have to be taken to the hospital.

Somehow I managed to stay curled up in the car, and as soon as we reached home, I jumped out and ran upstairs to hide in bed. I needed to recoup and be in good shape the following morning. We would leave by bus at 6:30 a.m. to go to the warm ponds and have our ceremony.

It did me no good to have some hot ginger tea in the evening before going to sleep. I still felt sick and tossed about. I only wanted to feel the safe steadiness of my bed, in the darkness of my room, with my eyes closed—and hope for the best for the following day.

## PART II: THE OTHER SIDE

The night passed. Then an alarm went off. But it was not my alarm clock. It was my stomach that woke me up at dawn, with the urgent need to make a dash to the bathroom and vomit. Nothing like that had ever happened to me before. I heard my friends being concerned about me. Someone gave me an antiemetic tablet, which I managed to keep in my stomach for only a few minutes.

That was too much. I went downstairs to seek some help, and there I found the Native American owl medicine woman. She took me to her room and hugged me. I was crying, and I was angry. I explained to her that it was no surprise for me to have seasickness, but the continual vomiting the following day was absolutely unreal.

While still holding me in her arms, she began to see in the darkness for me. "Yes, I can see. It happened in Atlantis. You were fourteen and were a member of the Council. You repeatedly warned, 'Change your ways or Atlantis will collapse!' But they did not listen. And you witnessed the destruction of your civilization."

Instantly, my diaphragm stopped bouncing, like a trampoline that stops wobbling as it finally realizes that no one is jumping on it.

Atlantis…I do carry cellular memory of my dear Atlantis. I was always interested in the so-called myths of old and avidly read about them. I was moderately interested in fairy tales for children, but I was absolutely fascinated by ancient civilizations and their gods.

Such was the trauma of witnessing the ruinous sinking of the glory and splendor of the most accomplished civilization of its times that I still cannot digest its failure, and I reject it with pervasive fear. But what was I doing in the Council at fourteen years of age? The owl medicine woman saw that I was so wise, even at my tender age, that I was worthy of being included among government advisers.

Now I got it. I had crossed half of the world to reconnect with my owl medicine woman, who saw in the dark for me, and to finally face an ancient trauma and my fears. That was what Hawaii was waiting for—to hug me back as a soul who had outgrown and dropped very old, very heavy energy.

Hawaii waited for me like a truly loving mother who is always there for her children whenever they need her.

I hopped on the bus, and we left for the destination that I had mistakenly thought would be the main feature of my trip. We reached the warm ponds before noon only to find that the park was closed for maintenance of the trees. "It's all perfect!" our group leader reminded us. So we waited and saw several visitors leave. Less than an hour later, the park reopened, and we were practically the only visitors there. We had the warm ponds all to ourselves for our ceremony! In addition, we were given beautiful flowers that another group had ordered and left behind.

We were a bit surprised at the temperature of the water, which was lower than expected. Some said that it was "Canadian hot." What had happened was that the tide had receded, dragging the warm water out to sea, and it came back bringing fresh, clean water for us.

Our ceremony consisted of each one of us, in turn, being kept floating still in the water while our group leader held our head and whispered prayers.

There was always time left to have some fun. I enjoyed swimming around a bit in the pool that was warming up and then sitting in the water having a beauty treatment by the little fish that were pecking at my legs, exfoliating my skin.

During the rest of the retreat, I felt the need to withdraw into myself to allow healing at all levels. I was not inclined to have a good time like the others were having while on holiday in one of the best destinations in the world. Besides, my guts needed some drugs to recover from the prolonged vomiting. I could not enjoy the food that was available anymore. I was in Hawaii, of all places in the world, but I badly wanted to go back home.

I wisely and obviously gave up the trip to swim with dolphins and instead went with a friend to the north of the island to visit a wild and sacred nature reserve. I was in awe when I reached the bottom of Pololu Valley. The cliffs, the roar of the ocean, and the lush green transported me to prehistoric times when the land was untouched, and few human inhabitants would roam it. I would not have been surprised to see dinosaurs come to the river to drink.

My friend and I wanted to say hello to the ocean when we arrived. It seemed the right way to behave in that sacred place. We held hands and stepped to the edge of the lapping waters. The ocean responded with a powerful wave that got our legs wet and sprayed all over us. We stayed in the valley until we felt we had absorbed enough energy from that magic place. Then we said goodbye to the ocean which, again, splashed us. How wonderful it was to see that the ocean heard our calls and responded to us with waves that were more powerful than normal.

The power of that ocean was a force of nature that I had never experienced before. Surging from the deepest and vastest waters in the world, and matching the winds and storms above, it is a force that deserves the utmost respect. In addition, you must be highly skilled if you decide to venture into it.

Isn't that a metaphor for our subconscious—for that vast sea in each one of us that our conscious mind cannot see in its entirety, nor can our eyes penetrate all the way to its bottom? That is, unless and until we meet it with love and respect and embrace it and accept it as ours because we ourselves added to it little by little. With courage, gentleness, and some skill, we begin to know how to navigate it, reaching places that we did not know were so near, whether we like them or not.

The ocean does not restrain its voice. Its size is matched by its roar. No one or anything can overpower that voice or shut it up. It is the voice of the billions of creatures that live in it and that, in turn, keep it alive, from the smallest to the biggest, from the transparent ones to the most colorful.

Voice—how important it is to have a voice, assert one's presence and existence, express oneself, speak louder if others pretend they can't hear, or join with others with one voice. I did know how important it was for me to be heard and to be approved of when I spoke, if not with words at home or at school, at least when singing melodies, both solo and in a choir. But I was not listened to when I attempted to speak, and I brought shame to my family when I sang, and earlier in life, when my mother shushed me so that I would not bother her or the neighbors. I had to keep my voice small and be extremely careful of everything I said to spare me additional hurt and trouble.

Constantly restraining myself and being overcareful at every move is no life, no freedom. It is like walking on a tightrope, sensing danger all around.

\* \* \*

Back home from Hawaii, I was excited to start working on the renovation plan of our newly acquired country house and get busy clearing its garden.

The following year passed without any particular highlights at work, but it presented me with an unexpected surprise toward its end.

## Chapter 24

The project of renovating our country house was big and demanding. However, we were not in a hurry to see the house sparkling and beautified with new plaster and color. We bought it to have our weekends away from the city and get our hands dirty, as a change from our work. We could take our time to renovate it in installments while setting money aside to see it finished when my husband and I would both retire in a few years' time.

We did very well to buy it in the first place but even more to buy it at the right time to keep us busy and interested just before and into the important transition in life that retirement is. The house itself had not been kept up for quite some time, nor had the garden. That played to our advantage because it kept the price low. No system was up to standards, and there was some asbestos to be cleared.

We planned a reconfiguration of the layout and use of rooms with an architect friend of ours.

Every weekend, we drove north to see how the works were advancing but most of all to clear the garden that had become quite overgrown. With time and patience, we could start planting vegetables, and when harvest time arrived, we were proud and grateful to pick our own home-grown produce.

A memory I had totally forgotten, almost repressed, came back to my mind. When I said to my father that I wanted to study horticulture, he curtly stated, "We are not landowners." No more discussion. When my husband and I bought our first home that had a vegetable garden, I consoled myself by thinking that tomatoes did not need me to have a degree in order to grow. Twenty years after leaving that house, the Universe led me again to own a garden and grow vegetables.

While standing in my garden and sensing the vastness around me, I thought I would have been happy indeed working in nature. Choices in life had led me through other paths; however, those paths turned out to be only a detour that eventually took me where I was attracted and destined to be—in nature, in the open air, tending to a vegetable garden. I looked forward to spending the weekends in an atmosphere that was the opposite of working at the office. I could do some manual work and breathe fresh air.

I had another two years and a few months to work, and then I would be due to retire, having reached retirement age and concluded thirty full years of service. In the meantime, time at work went by more easily than in previous years. Toward the end of the year, the headquarters repeated their offers for early retirement that had been launched the year before. I was not interested at first but was encouraged by my husband to at least read the email attachment. We sat down and did our calculations. I weighed the pros and cons other than money. What would I leave behind, such as human contact, and what would I gain that working from 9 to 5 prevented me from having, such as energy and time?

We decided that I should take the offer. I left the workplace with a happiness and pride that kept a smile on my face. No matter the nervousness of saying goodbye to all my colleagues from the lectern in the main lecture hall; my eyes did not well up.

I spent the following three months sleeping, recouping my energies. It was winter, and the long hours of darkness and the cloudy weather favored my rest. The severance that I received with my retirement made us comfortable to change the plans for the renovation of the country house. We could pay for work that would have otherwise been postponed. As time progressed, my husband and I developed the idea that such a big project could be turned into our main residence.

We would have to leave the city, our habits, and maybe our friends. That was a bit uncomfortable to contemplate. However, the renovation dragged along for three years due to problems with the contracting firm. Over those three years, we had the time to gestate within us the idea of moving away from the city to go and live in a tiny village.

Eventually, I could not wait to go.

We moved there one summer. All the while, I had kept the new house a secret from my brother to spare me from a rerun of what he had told me about an acquisition of my husband's at the time of Mother's death.

For the first time in my life, I lived in a house that my husband and I had molded to our liking and a space that we could truly call our own. The houses we owned before were all spaces we found already made, and we had settled in by adjusting to what already existed and had been built by the previous owners, according to their taste and the fads of their own time. But this one would give me a new sensation of ownership.

On a darker side, I sensed the clamp of the flashing thought that this would be my last home. But it did not last long. The happiness of living in a setting we both were attracted to, and experiencing that life here is more pleasant than it is in the city center, allows us to lean toward this place rather than what we had known before. We do not miss anything about the city.

The silence, the space, the greenery, the wild animals are all features of a setting that is more conducive to spiritual work. But most conducive to spiritual work and its effects was the freedom to use the whole day as I pleased. Granted, I had chores, but I no longer had the duty of the rote that gorged up ten hours of my day, which I could not shrug off when I was "free" in the evening and on weekends.

Twenty-nine years at work, plus three years at the university, plus sixteen years at school, forged a conditioning to set the alarm clock in the morning and frequently look at my watch to ensure I did not waste one minute. And when I relaxed, sometimes I took "relaxing" as my duty or piece of work, which I must finish within a certain time.

Letting time and clocks direct our lives is a ridiculous conditioning that keeps us from questioning its purpose. It ensures we do not give our attention to what is important in life. We let an external, fictitious authority govern our lives.

The spiritual work that I could finally do any day led me to the Emotional Freedom Technique (EFT), the tapping technique, which was very effective for my car sickness. The friend who accompanied me through this process understood that I am a Highly Sensitive Person (HSP) as she is, and I began researching this new concept.

For several years, I had known that I was an empath, but I had never known if that was of any use. I equated it with oversensitivity, which I regarded as a trait that makes my life, and sometimes the lives of those who come into contact with me, miserable or difficult at best. It made me feel guilty for restricting my parents' freedom to express themselves toward me.

But by reading the up-to-date studies on empaths, highly sensitive people, and vulnerability, I understood that I had an asset. For the first time in my life, my view of myself changed from faulty goods to rare merchandise. I learned that empaths very often are on the receiving end of narcissistic people. I found lists of traits of the narcissistic type that matched my mother's psychological profile down to the smallest detail, which led me to the notion that she had a mental disorder.

At sixty years of age, I found out about the existence of a scientific picture of what I had been up against since day one. In fact, since conception. I saw that my mother fed off my suffering, both physical and emotional. I saw that she used all my soft spots to ridicule me and make me feel ashamed of them. I saw that she destroyed my boundaries by ridiculing me for even attempting to put them up. I saw that she projected her dislikes onto me. I saw that she betrayed me by putting me on the spot in public, whether to ridicule me or overcompliment others by first putting me down or by telling me off for doing something that she had insisted I should do or had never told me not to do. And I saw how controlled she was by her fears and weaknesses.

All of that confirmed that I am indeed a survivor of child abuse, both physical and emotional. But the abuse was extended throughout my mother's life until her death when I was forty-nine. I was not a child any longer, but I was still emotionally abused.

Besides, there were psychological forces at play that attracted my mother into my father's family. The popular saying that "women marry their fathers" is also true for men. And so it goes that my father married his own mother. My mother was highly admired by many in the extended family, but in private, she was much more similar to her no-frills mother-in-law than could be seen in public. This was a dichotomy that I had noticed and observed since I was young. When she was lying in the coffin, someone asked me, "Was she always so elegant?" Yes, and even more with her pearl necklace and earrings and gold rings.

One day, I went to put some flowers on her grave. From a distance, I noticed that something was off. Along the row of stems that held the portraits of the deceased, my mother's stem was tilted forward, and her portrait was vertical instead of angled—like all others were, so as to be visible to visitors while walking. Although the stem was straight and intact, it was evident that it had been hit hard enough to tilt it and chip the marble base that held it in place. It was the only damage that I could spot in the rows of graves that I walked through.

My brother was sure that it had been done on purpose, but I refused to believe such outrage. However, my mind went back to a poisonous complaint letter that my mother penned and read out to me, addressed to the old man who had restored her chest of drawers; or to remember one of her last complaints to a shop assistant who just could not keep her mouth shut anymore, at which my mother was most surprised and to whom she gave a rose. My mother did not fail to let me know how much money that rose cost her.

In view of all I have become aware of, I can now say that it is not impossible that the damage was done deliberately.

\* \* \*

Spiritual healing occurs over time. Since it consists of work on energies, it is initiated by willing a change. Energy then shifts a bit at a time, according to a pace and speed that is most beneficial for the individual. The request for healing is answered, and the extent of the healing is for what the person requires at that particular moment in time. There are mechanisms in place that prevent healing from being felt too much too suddenly. Healing is an extension of love, and as such, it conveys only love.

Sometimes one does not feel that healing has occurred, but indeed healing is always received. It is up to the person's acceptance to be aware of the healing, maybe at a later time.

Human beings come to Earth with baggage of miscreations that transcend their awareness. Bit by bit, their lives remind them of the issues they have to transmute in this particular lifetime. When someone requests healing, it is not healing for the whole lifetime. The soul comes into incarnation, and it will feel the need for healing at various times and stages of its lifetime on Earth. This is what is compared to peeling an onion or clearing layer after layer. Various issues are faced, and their lessons learned, sometimes with the help of a healer, and sometimes the same issue needs to be dealt with over and over, each time at a deeper level.

This was the case for my being unwell on every trip that I went on, whether by suffering from motion sickness, getting a bad cold with a temperature, or some bad tummy trouble—or the whole lot together. I was determined to get to the bottom of the issue. I could not be the only group member who felt ill on every trip.

I sat down and let Spirit speak. The memory of me going to play next door and my grandmother looking for me came to my mind. *That is odd,* I thought. I remembered that memory very well, and I expected something that I forgot about to be the cause of my problem. Instead, the memory persisted. Then I understood that I had to become aware of its subtle, far-reaching consequences and the repetition of the same concept throughout my life with my parents, which forged strong conditioning.

When I was a child, I had to ask my parents, "May I go there?" As a little girl, I even had to inform my mother if and when I was going to the bathroom. And when I was no longer a teenager, I had to do as Cinderella did and get home by a certain time. This long-standing conditioning stripped me of the joy of going places, enjoying where I was going, feeling in charge of myself, and growing up as an independent being.

What a term "independent" is. It is not contemplated by narcissists. My mother would exclaim it to express how impossible it was to have me do things her way. I could not be independent. I had to be tethered and keep her informed of my whereabouts, even after I married. She would even check if what I said to her was true by giving a ring where I told her I had been.

Enough of that. I asked Spirit for the antidote thought that would set me free from the poison of "I may go but not enjoy." Or, in other words, my body may go, but my soul must stay.

The inspiration was a beautiful mantra that has been useful and effective for other issues too:

*I am sovereign, with self-validation. I choose to enjoy.*

I am the sovereign of myself, and what I do and how I do it can be validated by myself only. At the moment of choosing, I know that I have chosen what I will enjoy.

It worked pretty quickly. I have fully enjoyed my trips ever since, including a long visit to India, where spicy food is not totally compatible with my stomach.

But if that release was successful, another issue returned to be healed more than I thought it had needed. Maybe my relentless detachment from the old conditionings or some other energies going on in other dimensions caused the return of my mother's energy yet again. I was dismayed. Had I not done enough? Had I not detached enough or forgiven enough? I had cut the cords between us twice with Archangel Michael's sword. I forgave her and wrote her a loving letter. Why such persecution? What more was needed?

However, I was still adamant about not talking to her. Besides, it would seem appropriate to me if she started off by saying, "I am sorry" in the first place instead of just wanting my forgiveness. It was as if I had to do all the work both then and now.

Utterances like "I am sorry" or "thank you" or "please" were like swear words in our family. Starting off by screaming "Forgiveness, forgiveness!" would be the standard way to ask for forgiveness in our mother tongue, without any mention of being sorry. The countenance and tone of voice would be quite enough to show that the person was definitely sorry.

Besides, we had a contract, and spiritual contracts are fulfilled to the smallest detail. I do not see why she should feel sorry for doing her job.

However, behavior is not to be condoned, and I do not want to have anything to do with her. I have my hands full with forgiving myself for bringing all this onto myself. It is just and fair that she does her part and learns to forgive herself.

I had learned an affirmation that I used as soon as I felt her energy approaching me:

*I forgive myself; I forgive my mother; I ask my mother to forgive me.*

I repeated it until I felt her energy fade away. But it seemed that it was never enough, which was so disheartening. Again, no matter how much I did, it was never enough or good enough. With some effort and doubt, I thought of reinforcing such affirmation by adding an ending:

*I forgive myself; I forgive my mother; I ask my mother to forgive me and forsake me.*

I did not want to say something that went against the Laws of the Universe or that just does not make sense within the Law. But then I overcame my false sense of smallness and took the courage to say that affirmation in full, trusting that Spirit would have nudged me if it was not acceptable.

She came back for months, and for months, I kept repeating that affirmation until one day, I began it in my mind, but I felt that I could not complete it. It just felt like a stuck lever that needed to be left where it was, lest damage be done. She has not come back ever since, at least that clearly, but I suspect that sometimes she hides behind a memory that flashes up in my mind or perhaps behind a song she used to like and that I happen to remember.

I have no idea whatsoever why my mother wanted my forgiveness and why she wanted it so badly. It is my will to form no ideas or expectations at all in my mind as possible reasons why. I have asked the Universe to be told the real reason at the moment of reviewing this lifetime of mine, after I have laid aside this physical body. I trust that, at that moment, I will hear her own reason why, and I will accept it.

## Chapter 25

There are things in life that seem to take up a life of their own. As a matter of fact, they are agreed upon before incarnation, and you can take all the time you want to reach them but reach them you will. It was the case for me of singing and gardening, as well as *A Course in Miracles* (ACIM). I had read about this mysterious title with no author way back in the 1980s, and I wondered what it was.

I do not believe in chance, as by now, I know that everything happens for a purpose. That book stood out for me on a bookshelf in my mother-in-law's bedroom. I was there to clear her apartment after her death, and it came as no surprise to me that she owned a copy. She was a Christian Scientist and knew a thing or two about the power of the mind.

I endeavored to read ACIM and do all the exercises for a whole year, every day as it prescribes. I found it interesting, but I could not understand it well. In fact, I could not read more than one and a half pages at a time, and still, I could not quite make out what it meant. So, after reading it all from front to back, I put it on a shelf. It was 1994.

In the group of spiritual healing in Toronto, no one had read it or done the exercises, although they did know of its existence.

It was in 2017 that a friend in the group gave me two books, and both books had been written by students of ACIM. Both books set me back on Course, so to speak, and I took it up again and did all the exercises again. This time, so many years later and with a lot of spiritual healing accomplished, most of the concepts clicked immediately in my mind as if they were perfectly clear. This time, I could find resources on the Internet that supported my understanding of the teachings and gave me guidance on how to apply them in my life.

The retraining of my mind, based on ACIM, has been the bedrock on which the healing—still ongoing—of my emotions and triggers has rested. Sensing the energies emanating from ACIM, and the energies emerging when meditating on the "idea for the day" are like coming home for me.

I may have an advantage in believing what ACIM says because I have always trusted Jesus. In fact, I prefer to call him by his authentic name, Yeshua. I have always had an inner knowing that he was a good and balanced person and very knowledgeable indeed.

In my life, I have met two people who have remembered Jesus in some past lifetimes of theirs and disclosed that secret to me with some embarrassment. *Who knows?* I thought. Maybe I knew him too, but I have no conscious memory of that. Maybe I was just one in the crowds while he was preaching. For sure, I was not an apost...

*Bang!*

Something deeply buried exploded in my third chakra, and I had a vision of an explosion lifting a lot of desert sand. Indeed, why could I not be one of his friends, one of his inner circle? *Okay,* I thought, *let us deconstruct myths and lay down all false sense of humility.* My trust of Yeshua is such that it obviously derives from my cellular memory of him.

We were a group of people who followed this young man who made everyone feel better just with his presence. We were risking our lives under that regime and those traditional rules of conduct. But we knew that there was truth in what he taught, and we chose to stand by him and continue his ministry.

I find that straddling two—or should I say, several—worlds at the same time is a fun way of living. It is accepting that the human being is not just a small decaying body to which things happen and that you get one chance only. Accepting life in all its aspects is fun; it is freedom. Opening the mind simply means accepting the vastness that mind is. It is thrilling to surf the waves of dimensions and all possibilities once a solid base has been established to maintain perfect physical, mental, emotional, and spiritual balance.

There are lots of paths and healers to meet all needs of everybody in need of healing. What is most important is first to ask the Universe to send the best healer who operates with integrity and for the highest good of all. The more advanced one is spiritually, the fewer teachers there are and the more concealed they are. The old saying still holds: when you are ready, the teacher will appear. Nowadays, we know that this can be read as: when you increase your frequency, you will find a more advanced teacher for yourself.

My spiritual journey has led me to feel stronger. Feeling stronger means that I have seen some untruths in my life, and I have dropped them along the way. Of course, that has made me stronger because now I have less bulk weighing me down. Feeling stronger also means that I can withstand the resurfacing of memories that my subconscious had protected me from facing. Another way to put this is "peeling the onion of denial."

For years, I thought that my mother died feeling angry at me. But denial or maybe some guilt prevented me from applying to her what I had known all my adult life about other people—that when death is approaching, a person is no longer capable of controlling their behavior, and they end up showing their true colors. And, more importantly, people on their deathbeds do not lie.

So it became apparent to me that my mother did not die angry at me. In fact, she could not bear the sight of me. She could not stand my presence or maybe even my existence. It was only spontaneous for her to target me. With this realization, I fully understood all that Doreen had said that I suffered with my mother. She listed first of all rejection. Now I see that my mother did not want me; in fact, I suspect that, on top of that, she did not want to encounter my soul again, given the past experience we had together.

I found confirmation of "rejection" when I found again my notes of my first past lifetime regression, in which the purpose and terms of the present incarnation were seen:

*My mother is yelling as if she were crying, shouting, "No, no, I don't want it!" She does not want to be pregnant. She is in the master bedroom. I recognize the wardrobe and the mirror. She is standing, holding a handkerchief. She is turning her back to me. She says that she does not want me because it is an obligation— an obligation to procreate.*

*She lives being pregnant like having a pipe inside of her, running from her belly button up to her throat. It stops her from breathing.*

*I am so sorry for my mother. She lived having this foreign body inside herself really badly.*

*She shouts, "Set me free, my daughter!"*

*Spirit caresses the pipe, and shimmering diamonds cascade from it.*

*My mother is holding a ragdoll, and I am entering it. I wish my mother realized that she is holding a baby, not a doll.*

*My mother is still crying. She even becomes a child again. I need to become her mother to soothe her spirit. We jump together into magma, and when we re-emerge, I know that I am different.*

*My mother is standing in the doorway and smiles at me with malice. She is misbehaving; she runs away from me; she wants me to shout at her. She wants to suffer.*

*What do we need to live in harmony?*

*My mother breaks her glasses. Now she will see, albeit not clearly but with her own eyes.*

*I am an insect, swimming beneath the sea waves. Bit by bit, I am losing my insect attributes, and I turn into an amphibian. I can now breathe both in and outside the water.*

I remember the sense of peace that I experienced at the end of this vision, which gave me the certainty that my relationship with my mother had been healed once and for all. I was so wrong and so ignorant of the workings of the mind.

For many years in my young adulthood, I thought that school had been the worst period in my life. Along my spiritual journey, I became increasingly aware that my foundational years since day one set the tone for my way of behaving and reacting, for my choices, energy levels, and difficulties relating with others and living with my own personality.

Throughout my life, I noticed with some irritation that I encountered a "hateful" character wherever I found myself studying or working. At every stage of my life, I had to deal with at least one person at a time whose demands of me clashed with my soul, and I ended up seething with anger that I could not get rid of. Those people were all authority figures, such as teachers and bosses, though occasionally, some colleagues fell into that category, too.

I always blamed myself for not being easygoing and tolerant. I wanted to feel at ease with everybody, even though I knew that it was not possible, even for the kindest of people.

I wanted to have been born into a different family, with different group dynamics and different issues to clear. For many years, I thought that I would have gladly done without my mother and paternal grandmother. However, that is what I agreed to, and that is what I attracted—a lot of rage, judgment, and no love. In fact, the whole lineage has held the belief "I am unlovable."

With the years passing and forgiveness work, I have become more tolerant of others and their choices. After all, it is their life.

However, the detachment from busyness and respite that came with retirement were preconditions for becoming more tolerant and detached and less judgmental. Forcing myself to see things differently while I was drowning and gasping in overstretching, over-giving, overdoing with super-production and super-efficiency, was impossible because the timing and place were not conducive to wise decisions and change. A break was needed, as well as a bit of peace, to make long-time choices that would make a real difference in my mind and soul.

For many years, I asserted that I would have done without everything that happened to me and without all my mistakes and the shame attached to them. I could not see the silver lining, the gift in anything that I went through, whether by obligation, such as family members and school, or by choice, such as failing to become an opera singer. I am still stern, but I am relenting because I feel I am detaching from my past.

For many years, I wondered, where did I go wrong? Maybe with a little more effort, I could have done it, but I was not strong enough to go the extra step. I am sorry to say that I did my best, for my best has likely amounted to accruing more low-frequency energy that will need to be worked on.

My biggest fear is to have to meet again with my mother's and the godless high priest's souls, for such a huge bunch of shocks on me is likely to span over lifetimes, not just one. However, of one thing I am certain because I saw it: the vase on the head of my statue has fallen to the ground, and it is tilted and emptied out. I trust that this means "mission accomplished." At least, I do not need to suffer anymore.

I feel I am the "seventh generation:" the generation of souls incarnating in a lineage who come in with the mission to change things within the lineage. Something was very wrong with the way my ancestors lived their lives, and I was determined to return to the truth.

Anna, why do you do it? Because I want to be empowered and to empower others, beginning with the channels for conveying life on Earth—women.

# PART III:
# Merging the Sides

I was born with the courage to feel, and feel I did throughout my life. I have had the courage to watch and keep my eyes open. I have chosen to process all my experiences to glean wisdom and achieve freedom through forgiveness. I am now steady on my path to remembering who I truly am and focusing on creating a bright future for myself and the whole world. It *is* possible.

## Chapter 26

"The Earth is an experiment. That's what it is meant to be. It was the first completely free-choice planet; there's not one other because this was so successful. But this is the school of lessons, like a reform school. You come down, learn your lesson, love God, and go home. As the angels say, it's easy. Except it is not so easy because the lessons are hard. The thing is, we are down here, we are learning the lessons, we have experiences to add to our treasure chest of knowledge. (The truth of what we do is to experience Earth for Mother-Father God Who are so vast They can't individuate into a being, so we have to experience for Them). And the angels say, enjoy the journey. They want you to lighten up and laugh and enjoy the journey even though there are hard lessons.

"And the thing to remember is, you wrote your chart anyway. All the lessons in there, you wrote. You wouldn't have written them if you didn't think you would get through them. And you never get down so low that they don't pick you up. Never."

That's how Doreen summed up why we come to Earth and what it is all about. The lessons are hard, or rather, seem to be hard because we have forgotten what we decided to experience at the time when the Earth experiment was launched. Forgetfulness was needed to make the game seem real, but over the eons, its veil became so thick that we began believing that life in a body was the only reality. We wanted to experience what life without

God was like, and we ourselves have imagined millions of situations that are characterized by the absence of Love.

Creative minds we are in truth, not physical bodies, which are only vehicles that allow us to experience what would not be possible to experience otherwise, such as feelings and sensations. Humans have become more and more disconnected from the wisdom of the physical body that was developed over eons of time and kept us in harmony with the rest of nature. We have lost the awareness of our true identity through indoctrination and conditioning, not to mention manipulation, experimentation, and deliberate enslavement to programming that remote-controls our minds.

I cannot find suitable terms for the pain and frustration I feel at seeing how not just my own lineage but God knows how many thousands of millions of women—that is, millions of souls who experienced incarnation on Earth—were deliberately kept in obscurantism and taught fake truths that have made their lives, and indeed life on Earth, like hell. It was a snowball effect that started with the repression and stifling of a way of life that was in harmony with natural rhythms and forces and that grew into oppression and eradication to make sure that the natural forces would be considered diabolical, to be feared in terror, and eventually, turned into taboos.

It was not just a movement that was started by a few people who wanted to retain power over the masses. Not just humans but also other beings may choose not to serve the Most High. Some beings followed a "fallen" path of manipulation and untruth to turn human minds away from their source. However, in doing so, they do prod others to return to Light and Love!

There are many worlds with their inhabitants and many universes. The Earth is a coveted planet because of the creative power of the souls who incarnate here. We are indeed very powerful beings because Mother-Father God, Source, the Eternal, created us in Their image. That image is not a body with a head, trunk, and two arms and legs. It is Spirit, who holds all the attributes of its Creator—that is, eternal life, knowledge, love, peace, creativity—and retains them eternally.

The apparent death of a body is an illusion, just like suffering is. The human mind has retained a faint memory of its truth, having passed through experiences of lives on planets and star systems that have added to the baggage—but also to the treasure chest—that it carries around through conditioning, indoctrination, dogma, and trauma.

However, the very reason why so much effort and even cruelty is put into making sure that we never remember who we really are is that Spirit cannot be killed, no matter how much manipulators try to. Spirit will always remember its true essence and yearn for its return home, which is not a place. Instead, it is the full remembrance of its own identity.

There was a classmate of mine who was much appreciated by the philosophy teacher because she had the constant, bothersome thought that if God exists, then why is there suffering in the world? They would discuss it, while I just watched them and kept myself as unnoticed as a fly on the wall. I thought to myself, *Can't you see that God has nothing to do with suffering in the world?* My spirit, my guts were absolutely sure of what my mind was thinking. In fact, my mind held that thought because I knew it was true and felt it was true, but I could never have discussed it or found any argument to support it. To me, it was true, as simple as that.

Simple is beautiful and makes sense, but instead, for the vast majority, complicated is praiseworthy. Somehow, even back then, in the early 1970s in my teens, I had an inner knowing that there was something wrong with the way adults lived. It was complicated and perpetuated the same complication in the younger generations.

I cannot find suitable words to describe the ignorance of sexual matters in which women have been deliberately kept, to the point of labeling them as virtuous when they were as naive as delicate porcelain dolls. Having in my genes female ancestors who did not know what marriage was, how babies were born, or why they suddenly bled one day, is something that tugs at me. It makes me want to help those women, and many more, to change things and begin shouting that there is so much more that is kept from them. Many more untruths, unnecessary suffering, and dissatisfactions are waiting to be rectified and returned to their natural, God-given state.

We have come to Earth to rebalance our miscreations. I have very obviously come here to reclaim my own power, which I gave away by believing others rather than my inner guidance. They told me lies about myself based on their perception of their own state of mind and projections of the inner uneasiness they felt at my actions and words.

"What tree are you?" a psychologist asked me. I let my guts and heart shape an idea and said, "A ginkgo biloba."

She was surprised. She expected me to say an apple tree or a pear tree or maybe a sycamore like there were so many in the square below. But why a ginkgo?

"Because a ginkgo is ancient," I said, "and carries more wisdom than other, younger trees. It is poisonous, but that means it is medicinal too. And it shoots out of the ground straight toward the sky. It is not native here, so no matter how many trees it sees around it, the ginkgo stands alone, never among its own kin."

That's how I felt different most of my life, like a poisonous ginkgo biloba, whose healing effect would be acknowledged only in the long run. I was isolated from and even rejected by groups and never belonged until the awareness of reality dawned on me.

For many years, I could never forgive myself for believing my mother. I had no boundaries, and I could not put up any to avoid feeling doubly hurt when they were smashed down. But boundaries are an act of self-love and a means to maintain one's own integrity.

Empaths attract narcissistic and difficult types, which are their opposing energies, for the purpose of strengthening ourselves on many levels, inside and out. I chose my mother as the main contract of my lifetime because I knew she would not make a good mother. I chose to feel different, disempowered, and isolated.

My ginkgo medicine popped up fairly spontaneously every now and then, even at work, as well as at groups of spiritual healing and advancement. It comes naturally to me to encourage people in the direction indicated by the group leader in a well-meaning way. But not everybody is equipped with the same level of doggedness and courage with which I came to Earth to get through the energies that I had to relive in order to accomplish my mission.

I like to think that my feeling different and outposted is indeed part of my mission on Earth, which I took on like many tasks I have chosen—tasks that were waiting for someone to take them on, but no one else would volunteer for them.

For several years, I read the channeled monthly messages from Archangel Michael, with which and whom I resonated with deep love. So many times Archangel Michael would repeat, "You are the vanguard, the way-showers, the beacons of Light," but I did not understand what he meant because my ego doubted that those words were meant for all the readers of his messages, none excluded, and therefore for me too. The energy carried by those messages attracted my soul, and "energy attracts like energy" is a Universal Law. But my ego still made me doubt my own truth.

Nowadays, I hear and see that groups of spiritual healing and advancement are attended by young people in their twenties who feel the urge to change things and have come equipped with gifts that were rarely seen in my generation, not to mention before. I, therefore, like to think that I came to this Earth at a time when the fog of untruth was so dark and thick that few like me volunteered to pierce through it and anchor the Light so that more Masters of Light could navigate and flock here in large numbers.

I strove to be well-meaning and keep my integrity while toiling to survive in this environment that banned God's Love, and that is what made me feel different, unnoticed, and rejected. Many souls who encountered me on their path just could not see me because they did not contain the level of my vibration, while other souls were fearful of the Light and rejected me in fear. However, it is also true that I have felt safer by remaining unnoticed and transparent, and at other times, I did make mistakes. Perfection is not of this world, and if we are here on Earth, it means that we have some twisted energy to straighten out.

Somehow, I have always had an inner knowing that I came here in service to God. Like other aspects of my personality that I abandoned at some point but then found again along my path—like singing, gardening, and *A Course in Miracles*—service to God for the greatest good of all has reemerged from the jumble and rubble of my inner world. My ego, forever alert at safeguarding its survival and supremacy, has kept me doubtful about the wisdom of my choice of following a spiritual path and eventually writing down my memoirs. Do I really have the talent for that? Or is this choice of mine just another ephemeral whim that I take on as a fad or even a passion and then let fall by the wayside, like learning to play the guitar that was so much in fashion in the 1960s (albeit for boys only)? Or is it like other interests I felt stirred by and developed to a certain extent but never managed to turn into an occupation?

However, no energy is wasted. All I have learned in my life, all the hobbies I had, and all the skills that I honed have made me a more well-rounded persona, and I even suspect that somehow they have contributed to my spiritual level of advancement in ways that I cannot recognize clearly.

Doubting one's own capabilities is a program that the ego keeps running. The human mind goes straight to finding fault through a lot of comparison against others and self-judgment, and that is a trap that empaths fall easily into because they are particularly self-reflective. Since we are wired like that, we attract characters that are particularly keen to condition us into believing that there is something very wrong with us.

*A Course in Miracles* has provided me with a way out of illusion by reminding me of what the human mind has trained itself to repress. That path is simply a return to truth, and it has helped me to come out of low-frequency, dark energies, and even recurrent obsessive thoughts in a manner that is much swifter and more effective than any other method I have tried. It latches directly onto where the problem originated because "energy attracts like energy," that is, Love resonates with Love.

Love was the energy that I sought as a child but could not find. Love comes in many forms. It can be warmth, companionship, nurturance, protection. I needed the warmth from a heart that loses itself beyond time and extends and pours itself into another heart. I remember that need distinctly; it was a need in my heart for quenching its thirst. I witnessed a classmate of mine taking a moment off from our games to lie back on her bed and let her mother stroke her forehead and blonde hair and linger in that mother-and-child gentlest of connections, both of them totally oblivious to my presence. I watched them while observing that such a picture could not exist in my family because my proudly working mother did not have the time that my classmate's aristocratic non-working mother had.

My soul constantly needed to look up to someone and trustfully follow their example. I was ten when my brother invited one of his classmates home. I had heard him comment that this classmate was not very bright, but when I met him, I noticed that, unlike my brother, he was expansive, well-mannered, and not shy to express himself in a very pleasant, happy way that made him seem more adult than his adolescent age. I was pleasantly surprised. And, unlike other friends of my brother, who never even looked at me, this new friend took both my hands in his own and called me by my name. He said something to me that I no longer remember, but he said it with the intention of an elder toward a child that made my heart expand and look up to him as a trustworthy example to follow. In an instant, I understood how to grow up. What a wonderful example of life he was to me, even for that brief half minute. The nourishment that I gained from that connection has lasted me a whole lifetime. I have kept scanning for more such examples but eventually ended up with only two or three in my whole life.

If I had had him longer in my life, I would have known what nurturance is. Nurturance is a theoretical concept that I heard of rather late in my life. It is a beautiful form of love that lends attention and care to someone young so that they grow like a tree, with firm roots that convey healthy nourishment to the expansive, out-reaching arms along which the magic of creativity will shoot out peculiar gifts.

Sadly, nurturance is a scanty commodity in this world that tends instead to impose on children patterns of behavior that they must adjust to. However, change is coming, and the new generation is no longer conforming to this form of straitjacketing. I sense it is now important to become fully aware of the importance of parenthood in accompanying souls through childhood into adulthood. For too long, parents have made children and then complained that children come with no manual of instructions.

There is indeed a manual of instructions for living life on Earth, and I encourage my readers to seek it. "Doctor, heal yourself" is a wise, old saying that tells us very clearly that before taking care of others and, before becoming able to take care of others, one has to take care of her/himself. Remember the instructions that are given on planes: always put on your oxygen mask first before helping others to put on their mask. Only when you are fully in your strengths can you begin to help others. This is self-care, and it is a major example to give children for them to develop self-respect and self-esteem. As a consequence of that, parents will earn their respect and esteem and will become examples that their children will look up to.

My mother was deeply convinced that she had done everything she could to make me happy. But "done everything" entails effort, and when effort continues, it becomes stress and even sacrifice, which fuel grudge. "Being" is its opposite. When one loves herself/himself, the flow of love extends to others effortlessly.

The parents' energy is the invisible backpack that children keep on carrying on themselves. Parents who think that worrying and telling their children to be careful and not to do this and not to do that are signs that they care are mistaken. In that way, they extend no love to their children. Their children will carry only their parents' worry and fears in their auric field. But if the parents trust themselves, they will trust their children, too. By greeting their children with "Have fun!" their energy of love will follow their children as happiness. Their children will feel loved and nurtured by their parents wherever they go.

Deep healing is required when the fears of the ancestors are passed to children through DNA. The image of the circle of kings was indeed the accrued fear of sex that came to me through my maternal lineage. As for my father's side, one day a thought was slipped into my mind like a message into a mailbox: there is incest in the lineage. Spirit told me that it is ancient, but still it remains in the lineage, and I am determined to transmute it because it was child abuse, too.

The dream of me hugging a tiger meant that my soul would be mauled if I attempted to look at a frightening issue that I was literally "embracing"— that is, sexual love. My soul got mauled when I saw what happened to Black Jaguar and me.

## Chapter 27

**Trigger Warning:**
**This chapter contains descriptions of sexual violence, which some readers may find distressing.**

Black Jaguar was a young man full of energy and could make love by experiencing it fully, sensing it in every fiber of his body, while his heart and soul would soar and expand. It was natural to him to have sex as a Divine experience. He was born that way. He was happy and content with himself and knew that he was living life in the way that was meant to be. It was as simple as that. He emanated an aura of loving pleasure that could be felt by whoever happened to be in his presence, including those passing him by. Perhaps girls and women would look at him in a way that was a bit different than they did at the rest of the men in their tribe. Jealousy and envy grew, especially in the heart of the high priest who saw in Black Jaguar the connection to the Divine that he just did not have. He knew he was not nearer the gods, as the people believed he was.

So the high priest and his self-serving assistant schemed an unnecessary need for a sacrifice to which Black Jaguar was called as if the gods had chosen him and, therefore, he had to feel honored and proud for being the one to be chosen.

The unnecessary torture to which Black Jaguar was subjected was sheer extermination, as their perpetrators meant its effects to last for eternity. It was not just the pick that gashed his body; it was the intention of extermination driving the pick again and again that gashed his subtle bodies and nervous system and that changed his natural current of love into a current of fear in all its aspects.

Twenty years of healing practice following the vision of Black Jaguar have given me a certain clarity of what happened both to him and to myself in parallel ways. First of all, Spirit cannot lie. What I sensed during the vision of Black Jaguar was not only written down in notes but also branded in my memory because it reemerged as the truth of what went on. Black Jaguar was intentionally exterminated solely because his sexual energy was Divine.

My mother did not wait for me to grow teeth naturally. Spurred by her aversion to toothless mouths, she took me to a doctor to whom she felt connected. This doctor saw the opportunity to exterminate an innocent, happy baby by wielding her power over the subconscious of a mother, as well as latching on to the mother's distorted sexual drive, thus making sure that the new generation would be like the two of them. In fact, worse than them.

For my mother, having and giving injections was like a rite of passage, an initiation, a sign of belonging to a level of humans that was more honorable than the rest. It meant truly belonging. It was she within the family who drove the habit of having injections because only this way of administering chemical substances would ensure good health in the human body. Nature did not suffice and could not be trusted. Nature is out to get you. A baby healthily growing in a home where two salaries and one pension ensured good and sufficient food, clothing, and protection for both adults and children was not enough for someone who had been cured by her own mother since her dad's tuberculosis was diagnosed.

My mother giving my brother so many injections, as he did not mind at all while instead I would run and scream and wrestle, made me ask myself a question, a legitimate one: what illness did my brother have, or even what did I have for her to give us that number of chemicals in that form? The answer is: nothing. Nothing. Injections were solely a way to appease a need of hers and a deep conviction that we would be strong only in that way.

To me, injections were a sign that I was very ill indeed. Pills did exist in those days, but evidently, I was among adults who did not believe that pills dissolved in baby food would be swallowed and not spit out. Medicines had to be pushed forcefully into the body in order to have a sure, visible effect.

Black Jaguar was subjected to that unnecessary torture repeatedly so that the deep wound would be forever reopened and never heal.

When I became slightly ill with a light temperature, and the pediatrician ordered a blood test, she told my mother that the levels of white globules in my blood could turn into leukemia. My mother told me that when I was an adult, with a pitiful whining voice that meant, "I was scared."

I have seen my mother get very irritated when other doctors proposed courses of injections for me, and after I produced a stream of tears, they caved in and changed the treatment. She was angered at me for having the upper hand over golden opportunities that were presented to her. So, scared as she may have been that time, the Black Jaguar that I saw and sensed from the point of view of Spirit confirms to me that the long courses of injections that the godless high priest ordered were unnecessary or at least way out of proportion to what I actually had.

The true purpose of those medical treatments was to exterminate my sexual energy for eternity. Thousands of other children were subjected to similar treatments like me, and I have wondered for decades if they ever made a connection between those treatments and the happiness of their sexual life or lack thereof.

The difference in the outcome of such experiences for babies and young children depends on their mission in life and on their parents' energy—especially their mothers, as it was mothers who took them to visit that doctor while dads were at work. And the janitor was well aware that the length of the courses prescribed by that pediatrician would surely scare children, as she hinted to my mother.

Interestingly, my brother became a doctor, as did my mother's brother. I felt lower than my brother because all I managed to achieve was to become numb. However, he was never washed the way I was. Of course, I do not know anything about his or anybody else's sexual life, as sex is never to be talked about. Illnesses and medical treatments are a common topic as much as the weather is, but sex is kept very private and very occasionally whispered about. It is never talked about like other natural needs—that is, pleasures such as eating and drinking—because it is not to be regarded as a permitted pleasure.

"Sex" is talked about by dropping remarks, whispering and giggling, and giving looks and commenting. It is staged in movies, and circulated as lust and porn on the Internet and in magazines. That is purported and understood as the only type of sex that exists and the only practical ways to learn about it.

But where is the God-given natural energy that effortlessly leads to ecstasy? What about the circulation of sexual energy throughout the organs that replenishes the whole body and soul and turns on our remembrance of our Divine true essence? Through sexual pleasure and ecstasy, we remember we are Divine. We remember our true essence by letting the natural energy inside of us connect to the Divine Who put it there.

That's what the powers-that-be have never wanted us to remember: that we can live perfectly happy and healthy because we are connected to the Divine. An incarnate soul who knew as much was put to death, but not without torturing her body first, in an attempt to suck or steal the secret of her powers, as well as for imprinting her cell memory never to be so beautiful ever again.

I have heard that people in sexual healing groups say they are wary about showing sexual pleasure to partners because they still fear that they will be persecuted for that.

What freaked me out about injections was not only the number and repetition of the treatments but, first and foremost, the subconscious energies and drive that my mother carried. I, as an empath, could sense them so clearly and her face screamed them clearly as well.

The cell memory of the torture that was perpetrated to Black Jaguar over an extended period, the daily multiple washing and changing of nappies while lying defenseless on my back, and the injections to allegedly do what nature was unable to effect have all set the tone for me to know that my mother would pull my panties down in order to inflict permanent damage on me. On top of all that, she ridiculed me all her life as silly for my fear, as well as for the size that she imagined my bum was.

I have lived the whole situation as rape and sexual assault, topped with emotional abuse, ever since I was a baby. It was meant to be castration and extermination for Black Jaguar, and it was meant to be extermination for me, but since I am female, I could still have sexual intercourse and get pregnant, even without sensing pleasure.

The practice of having to let my mother do whatever she deemed necessary on my body was such that I reached the point of knowing that I would have let a rapist take advantage of me without reacting in any way at all—not a sound or a defense movement, let alone running.

No matter how much healing practice I have done over the years, I still have to reckon with what Spirit said at the end of the vision of Black Jaguar: "The wound is much deeper than you can imagine."

I know that, as yet, I have never seen or comprehended the full extent of the damage that my mother, plus whoever she put me in the hands of, inflicted on me, and by that, I mean both the sexual terrorism and the emotional abuse. It would be far too much for my system to see all at once. It would probably send me into mental imbalance. I need the patience and perseverance to dismantle it, maybe even "one molecule at a time," and just keep steadily on the path of healing.

The sense of connection resides in the second chakra. It is not surprising, then, that I kept seeking ways to belong. My sense of belonging was destroyed along with the devastation of Black Jaguar's second chakra.

As a consequence of living among those energies, I have been seeking and praying for safety. Feeling safe is what my nervous system and memory have been seeking first and foremost. *A Course in Miracles* has indeed provided me with the sensation of a perfectly safe home within me. The unsafe family atmosphere that I was born into and grew up in was a continuous prodding for me to look within for the love I could not find around me. However, it takes time, in fact years, for a soul to understand that.

My mother and the other adults in my family may have "loved" me, but they did not contain within themselves a natural, unspoiled flow of love.

The window in the room of their childhood's heart was closed. No fresh air could flow in and keep the air in their heart constantly scented and nourished with love. The door of that room was shut, too, and no communication was possible.

I realized that I never had the loving presence of a grown-up soul who would take my hand and lead me through and out of situations that frightened me as a child in a way that would let me feel enfolded safely in their experienced, knowledgeable strength. They could not do that because they themselves had not gone through such experiences. They gave me what they had received: *Don't be silly. Stop that! What's all that about? Think of something else. Was that necessary?* And so those unloved little children, frozen at those moments in time, never stopped crying in dark corners of their subconscious, throughout the life of their growing, aging body.

We all have many children inside of us who are waiting for us to treat them right and heal them from their traumas, big and small, one-time and continuous.

I have prayed with the aim of creating "a loving, nurturing mother in a nightgown" for another lifetime. That picture sums up my wish for a mother who is good to children and sets an example for them of a fulfilling sexual life.

Now I know all too well that what I have been shaped into has not happened to me alone. Lots of women of my generation and before were treated in ways that turned them into unhappy adults. In my case, it is clear that my lineage, and not just my mother, contained the programming to perpetuate the pattern of sexual misery. Different generations had different ways and tools to keep on running the same old programming and make sure that its effects were firmly in place to secure its effectiveness on the next generation.

Even the way words were used is interesting for the purpose of understanding how sex was viewed and to be viewed. "Orgasm" was a term that was not infrequent to hear in my youth and when my mother was young, too. It was commonly used to indicate a state of frenzy or being frazzled caused by too many things to think of, too many requests all at once, and an unbearable pressure to do them all in a flurry and hurry. Indeed, orgasm was something that decent ladies never would have and never had. I welcome the term "ecstasy" that is now used for the state of Divine bliss that the acme of sexual pleasure truly is.

When the first studies on sexuality were carried out, terms like "frigidity" were minted. I welcome the replacement of such a term with the current term "numbness," which allows for the connotation of a need for self-defense from unbearable memories—both emotional and physical.

At its opposite, "nymphomaniac" was the label for women who were regarded as having insatiable sexual appetites. Some men may have also been called womanizers or even satyrs, but that was taken as a compliment for their virility. Now the appropriate term "sex addict" encompasses all sexes when there is a need for psychological help, just as with any sort of addiction.

And what about the term "masturbation," which smells of medical jargon? Calling it "self-pleasuring" is indeed calling that act by its own name, wrapped with the same love that it carries.

In the early days of my search for healing, I became more and more aware of the importance that touch has on imprinting memories in the physical body. I, therefore, termed "mishandling" the collective loveless ways in which I was touched as a baby. The purpose for touching a baby's body as well as the feeling toward the baby who is being touched are the energies that are passed through the hands of the adult into the body of the baby. Babies grow very fast, and that fast growth is not just due to food. It is due to all the energies that surround the baby.

It is not enough to smile at the baby. It is the energy within the adults that connects to the energy of the baby. If the adults' energy does not contain love, it will be loveless energy that the baby's energetic bodies will sense and pick up. Most likely, this will make the baby scream or be triggered at a later time like a clockwork timer device.

All my life, I have been terribly ticklish on my sides near my waistline. When tickled, I laugh hysterically, when actually, I am unable to breathe due to anxiety. The muscular tension in my sides most likely originated from when an adult would pick me up and strip me naked. I froze with tension at the anxiety of being mishandled yet again without love and probably with disgust, too.

I had a nanny when I was a baby. The only thing that my mother ever told me about her—and kept repeating in public all her life—is that she said that I had a bum that reminded her of a certain film starlet of that time who was particularly curvy. Only once did my mother mention that she was eighteen, but she never told me anything else about her—a woman whom my mother and my family entrusted with their own baby. I never knew where she came from, why or when she left, whether she loved me or was happy working with me, or if she took up just any job that required no education.

I found a photo of the two of us. Neither of us is particularly happy. And I saw immediately where my earliest mistrust of wide-apart eyes originated.

## Chapter 28

I began talking about what bothered me with a psychologist when I was in my forties. Before then, I had sought help from doctors and therapists only to achieve orgasm, but I did not talk about my family dynamics because I was sure that they did not matter. I was seeped in the belief that I had lived in a perfect family and that my touchy character, shortcomings, fears, and failures were entirely my fault. I was so ashamed of them that I bottled myself up.

If I happened to mention the behavior of my family members, it was only to show that I did not manage to comply with their requests or achieve what was expected of me within the family and in society. But that was enough for one of the therapists to remark, "You had it rough with your parents," to which I reacted in strong disbelief. That remark remained stored in my memory, collecting dust waiting to be proven right one day or wrong and be tossed out.

With the passing of time, the accrual of bothersome behaviors by my mother and father became very irritating. When I ended up visiting another therapist upon the advice of a trusted friend, I began disclosing their behaviors because I really could not stand them anymore. However, I still firmly believed that it was me who had a difficult character and was incapable of being happy with my parents, happy to fulfill their requests, grateful for their guidance and teachings, or accepting of their "no" for an answer.

I began telling the therapist about the way my mother washed me and other behaviors that could have a sexual connotation. Very often, when I stopped talking, she would lift a stack of papers that was on one side of her desk and move it to the other side of the desk, then pick up the same stack of papers and move it back to where it was before and maybe move it once again. *What the heck is she doing?* I would think.

It took me twelve years after I had my session with Doreen and recovered from pneumonia to see that grabbing and plonking a stack of papers was her way to blow off steam from the heavy emotions that my stories caused in her. It was her way of feeling for me.

What is more is that I started talking about what had happened to me only thirty-odd years later. So much time elapsing between what happened and talking about it is an unequivocal sign of sexual abuse as a child. The abuse was so early and shoved in a strongbox of shame that it took me decades and a lot of courage to start talking about what bothered me, often not even realizing that it had been, indeed, abuse.

Those were the years in which I became acquainted and then familiar with Archangel Michael's channeled messages, and the time when my energy levels began plunging to an all-time low and stayed there for more than two years, causing a state of permanent anxiety. I like to think that Archangel Michael knocked on my door and presented himself because he knew I would need his protection in the coming years. Thank God, I accepted his arrival. I would need no less than Divine assistance to pull me through and pick me up again.

I was coming out of a patriarchal, wounded masculine view of the world in which I had felt much more comfortable than I did in the company of girls or women. Even though I had gone through the movement of feminism in the 1970s because I thought it was a welcome change, I did not deepen my knowledge about it. As soon as I witnessed the dynamics within a feminist group sparking anger and conflict, I decided that shouting in revenge against men was not necessary or meaningful for me.

However, I became aware that many posters advertising various kinds of products by displaying female nudity were purposefully geared to attract attention and sales and that was demeaning of women and the female body.

## PART III: MERGING THE SIDES

But I was still happy and unconcerned when someone proposed to make me "an honorary man" in an all-grown-up boy group.

I never liked patriarchal, macho humor because I felt it was vulgar, and I probably took after my own parents in that regard. But, in general, I was still laughing at the jokes that involved women as unbearable nags and did not react when hearing men curse Eve. I began to understand women's empowerment relatively late in my life, and that is certainly due to the fact that I have had many more lifetimes as a man than I have had as a woman. My freedom of action and expression is too strong a drive for me to incarnate in female bodies and suffer repression both in society and within the family.

But the time has come. Time is up. Now I know what it means to be a man—to be free to be concerned only with societal duties and seeking and obtaining some prominence and leaving all family duties to women, whether they like it or not. With an aim to make them like it and feel important and indispensable, men fabricate circular-reference praises, such as "I would be lost without you," thus turning the key in the padlock of the cell.

Patriarchy has kept women repressed because they knew that women's souls and minds are very powerful indeed. It is my assumption that the fear that patriarchy displayed during the insurgence of the feminist movement had among its causes the fear of old-style men that they would be treated the same way as they had treated women all along.

But in order to change the world, we cannot use old weapons. That would only lead to a bitter clash. Besides, those weapons would not be as effective in the hands of women as they would be in the hands of those who have wielded them for centuries. We need to use our own assets, no matter how they may be regarded by the souls who still cling to the old paradigm.

Our vulnerability, our willingness to show emotions, is one of our greatest assets. It makes us strong. Our sensitivity is another one of our assets because we know instinctively what is necessary—no need for questions or committees to find out. Our tendency to fall back on ways to live that are in harmony with nature and the pagan knowledge of old are pathways that can liberate us from cunningly imposed shackles so that we may begin building a new kind of society for the benefit and happiness of all people.

I worked in an organization where women were all in secretarial positions to help men who were all in executive positions. Starting this century, there has been an effort within such organizations to promote the hiring of women. Progress is being made slowly, and the hiring of a woman to the top level of an organization still makes headlines as the very first instance of such an occurrence. Some time is still needed to pass before such appointments will lose that connotation of newsworthiness which, I suspect, conceals resistance to change.

But before a woman becomes a member of society out there, she first has to grow as a healthy, happy baby, then become a sound girl. Then she may begin to have a role in a family and in society after having built solid foundations as a knowledgeable person who is well-prepared to give nurturance to whomever or whatever she chooses and agrees to help grow.

We must heed and honor the Divine Feminine within every one of us—all genders included, as everybody has an inner feminine side. Only in this way can a person soundly develop into adulthood out of a baby and a child.

A feminist slogan that was very popular when I was young was "I am my own," meaning that my body is my own property and no one else's. Only I can do with it what I want, and I won't allow others to manage it. In other words, women had the right to decide if and when to have sex, if and when to have children, if and how to have an abortion, and would not allow the use or displaying of the female body as an object or merchandise.

Women, as the human beings they are, had to start from the visible part of themselves—the body—to build a movement for asserting their own rights. Indeed, the use of their bodies and the way that the female body was considered for thousands of years of patriarchal thought and governments wounded their souls and dignity.

Now that the Goddess is coming back from her eclipse, and it is safe enough for Her to shine again Her light, it is a favorable time for women as a collective to reawaken to their dignity and power if they want to change the world. They can build a new society, a new Earth that rests on its own innate strength: the connection with the Divine and the recognition of the sacredness of all life.

## PART III: MERGING THE SIDES

Bringing a child into this world is the most sacred endeavor of all. Parents engage in a commitment that will take up most of their time and effort for two decades in order to ensure that the new generation will have solid foundations to live fulfilling and healthy lives and be capable of teaching the next generation by example so as to ensure the continuation of happiness and peace.

Among the confidences that my mother disclosed to me, she told me that she gasped in fear at hearing her first baby crying just after giving birth to him. I wonder how many women have reacted in a similar way, having had a baby instead of healing their subconscious first. It is clear that women do need to be helped, understood, and supported in every possible way to form their personalities and so enable them to make the choices that feel right in their own hearts. Societal requirements and pressure by family members or religion must be discontinued. Each human being must be left free to pursue their own path, having been freed from conditioning, constriction, and ancestral karma. The de-conditioning of the human mind is the first step toward a brighter future.

So many women have not wanted to have children deep down, but they could not even bring that thought to their conscious mind or they would have committed a sin. They would have been excommunicated by their religious community; they would have been disowned by family. They could not express their fear of carrying a baby within their body and sensing so many changes in the functioning of their bodies, nor their fear of childbirth and its consequences.

Ignorance of who we truly are and how we function naturally is the first virus that keeps us lost in life and prone to all kinds of unhappiness and trouble.

In my quest for learning about healthy sexuality, the first notion that struck me was the sacredness of the womb in all of its anatomical parts. That was a revolutionary way of viewing that part of my body and indeed of the body in general. The womb is the place of gestation not just for babies but also, and much more often, for ideas. The body's womb is the microcosm that parallels the Universe's womb of creation from where celestial bodies are brought into manifestation.

My body tingles when it senses the effect of the thought that the womb is the place where ideas develop, not the brain. Ideas and creativity cannot be the product of just logical thinking. They would lose in vitality, scope, purpose, and benefit.

Learning how the female body works and what the various anatomical parts of the womb are for revealed to me some facts that are not commonly known, such as that women do ejaculate. That fluid was regarded as sacred, as was menstrual blood in some ancient civilizations. Another fact supported by anatomy is that the first purpose of sexual intercourse is pleasure, not babies. But the most surprising notion I found is that childbirth is meant to be not just painless but even orgasmic. I resonate with this notion directly in my heart and womb, bypassing all logical scientific thinking—that is, all human scientific thinking. I know very well that "miracles" and "magic" are indeed based on scientific knowledge that the human mind has not attained yet and never will if it strips that knowledge of its inherent sacredness.

The re-emergence of ancient knowledge is not just due to the rediscovery or reinterpretation of ancient books or traditions. It comes from Spirit, our eternal essence, who we truly are, living in Oneness, Love, and Truth. Knowledge and wisdom are tapped through Spirit. Knowledge and wisdom are never lost and are eternal. As such, they remain untouched and unchanged.

Accepting the fact that we are spirit and are eternal is a step on the path of living life on Earth happily.

However, in order to keep walking steadily on that path, *A Course in Miracles* has provided me with the foundational training for remembering step by step that we are energy, or as the ACIM calls it, "minds." There is a very precise set of laws that need to be re-learned for us to live happily and create more happiness consciously. Ignorance of those laws has made life on Earth hell. It could be believed when my father used to say that, "We are born to suffer," but it is exciting news that there are instructions on how to live happily.

The very first idea in my mind that I needed to accept again as true was

## PART III: MERGING THE SIDES

that God is good. Only by knowing who God is and why and how She-He is good could I relinquish the image of God that was set through indoctrination and false beliefs. That was the bedrock on which all the following teachings in ACIM became readily accepted.

We are living in a time when dishonesty and many lies and untruths are disappearing and dying out, never to be accepted again. As the old paradigm is decaying around us, I have a vision of conceiving and gestating the new me, the true me, the eternal me, thanks to the guidance that is being offered from many parts. I choose to heed the signs that nudge me to accept certain types of guidance that are on the same path as I am and that I resonate with. No matter the kind of life I have had in this lifetime and that Black Jaguar had, I know that I can rely on my eternal truth and choose differently.

I have not had any children in this lifetime, and I am happy about my and my husband's choice. I have been far too busy healing my heart and soul to engage in an endeavor as gigantic as raising children. I knew I would not be able to support them at the time of their difficulty, especially when confronted with problems at school or with doctors. But with the retraining of my "mind" and by learning the laws of creation, I am sure I could do a good job, just as anybody could. Another time.

Then I will teach daughters from an early age about the sacredness of their role as vehicles of life on Earth so that they learn the truth of who they are and what they can do. I will help them grow self-assured, skilled, and knowledgeable about the facts and needs of life, so that they grow in Love and nurture with Love in their turn.

My vision for the future is a sacred mother-daughter relationship, which must first be based on a sacred relationship with and within oneself.

## Chapter 29

Along my healing path, I chose many methods that I resonated with, which I thought could help me out of my state of unhappiness. A recurrent instruction that every one of those modalities included gently prodded me again and again: love yourself unconditionally.

At first, I could only hear those words in my ears, but they could not reach my heart. It was an instruction that I did not know how to implement. It is hard, too hard, to love all parts of myself, including my irksome traits, my mistakes, my shortcomings, and above all, my choices for this lifetime.

If I closed my eyes and visioned myself as "loving" my inner child, all I could see was a little girl almost dead, unresponsive, lying on a poor bed, with me beside her, thinking to myself, *I don't know what to do to love myself back to life*. I could only sit beside her and wait. Such a vision appeared in my mind's eyes for a long time. For years, I could not feel forgiveness or, even less so, love for myself. And yet I knew that loving myself, all of myself, was a lever that would finally open the flow of abundance and bring me opportunities.

The lack of self-love kept me stuck in lack. It seems only logical and obvious that the examples I had in my family of origin were of that inclination, as I was attracted by that wavelength into their midst to change that frame of mind. I, therefore, needed to find a way to re-feel and re-fill love for myself.

A memory came to my mind, with a clear image of a small campfire. I was in a small clearing surrounded by a forest. I felt the protection of the forest, like a watchful spirit that holds space and whispers, "All is well now." The fire was the ritual to return to every night. It is night. Sit down and rest. Let memories free to emerge from within you, the long-forgotten ancient stories to be welcomed again like long-lost friends.

I was immersed in an air that was holding a quiet, soft space for me to begin my return to loving myself in all my aspects. I was there in my sixties, the age that I am now. I was there as a baby, asleep in one of my arms. And I was there as a little four-year-old, whom I was holding by the hand. I was set on my intention of finding love within my heart and letting it flow down my arms into those inner children of mine, to wake up the baby and let the little girl smile again.

A faint rustle from the foliage to one side signaled to me that a roamer was attracted to the energy emanating from the scene. I turned my eyes, and the long-lost friend appeared. Black Jaguar. Unmistakably you, Black Jaguar, with your horrible scar on your lower abdomen as if stitched by a surgeon. Twenty years on, Black Jaguar, it is you! You have been on my mind all this time. I wondered what had happened to you all these years, how you survived or maybe transitioned.

He kept looking at me, with his pale green eyes peeled and full of intention to reconnect with me, conveying all his strength into my heart. His heart was speaking to me through his eyes, which were the pale, emerald-green shade of feline eyes.

Twenty years more burden his body, heavy and older; it was not the body of a warrior or hunter anymore. It was the body of a man who had been stopped from running free and had been forced to sit and feed himself with food within easy reach. A man whose attention turned inward into his own mind, far from the pursuits of young age or for the benefit of his community. He was forced to be in the company only of his own thoughts and to survive on his own in the forest of life as a wounded, crippled inhabitant, thus risking being easily overpowered and falling prey not just to other forest inhabitants but also to despondency and listlessness.

I deeply honor you, Black Jaguar. Your will and skills of survival for such a long time in the forest of life are proof that you are like a very powerful jaguar

## PART III: MERGING THE SIDES

indeed. You are a unique, variant black jaguar with a heart ever-replenished with power no less than Divine, unabated, and unrelenting in the courage to keep on living under unimaginably adverse conditions. You walk all the way to and through places where others do not dare set foot, not even in their own minds.

Welcome back, Black Jaguar. Come, sit down with us, and hold my hand. Help us love ourselves again.

We closed our eyes and let the current of love trickle along parched channels to revive our souls.

\* \* \*

My husband is a great cook. He enjoys cooking, and we both enjoy eating, and so do our friends, who readily accept our invitations to lunch, knowing that they will eat something unusual and yummy. I never fail to thank him for cooking before every meal. Finding lunch ready and prepared by someone who puts love and creativity into it is a daily gift, and I know from experience how valuable it is. It is an intake of love extending through thoughtfulness and the pleasure of sharing.

Since he is the cook, he is also the one who buys groceries. I always present ourselves as, "He is the cook, and I am the housekeeper."

We tend to eat meat twice a week, and when lamb meat becomes available in spring, we buy it because we like it very much. One day, my husband came back home with the groceries, which I took out of the shopping bag to put in the fridge and pantry right away. Immediately, I noticed that the lamb meat stank to high heaven, while he had not sniffed anything.

All the meat we had bought at that shop for years had always been good quality, so we decided to cook that piece of lamb and see if it was good to eat. As we cut the first piece of meat on our dishes, both the smell and the taste were really bad, and we threw it into the trash.

The following week, my husband told the butcher what happened. The butcher said that he had not noticed either and that probably the cause was that the vacuum package was somehow pierced. So he gave my husband a piece of meat for free.

As my husband and I were finishing our meal, I remarked that the butcher was kind enough to trust us and that it wasn't just a trick to have an extra meal for free. My husband smiled at me. "Oh, come on, Anna. He *said* he did not notice!"

My body chemistry changed for the worse. My brain started fizzing, my legs lost all power of support, my whole body felt hollowed, and my levels of self-esteem plunged to the floor. Again, it happened again. Again, I naively believed lies. My husband had already left the lunch table and gone to his armchair. I was unable to move, resting my elbows on the kitchen table, holding my head in my hands, panting with my mouth open.

In my mind, I heard a soft noise and saw the air moving in the entryway to the kitchen as if leaves were being parted by gentle hands. Black Jaguar was back. He had sensed my energy change. His green eyes radiated with love and deep knowledge of what had just happened. He came near me, gently took my face in his hands, and kissed me on my forehead. Then he looked at me again. Without speaking one word, his full connection with my heart and soul through his feline eyes and powerful heart poured into my mind the light of knowing that that was the last time I would believe liars and their lies.

He came to me as he sensed clearly that particular turning point in my energy. A point of no return. To him and to me, that turning point opened the door to our freedom.

It will take me time and quite a few goes to rub away the responses of hurt, self-loathing, and incurable daftness in my third chakra that many years of "never seeing it coming" have made automatic. However, I trust I will make progress in that sense. When we incarnate to live on Earth, we come equipped with everything we need to work through all challenges in this lifetime, which includes a guidance system that will signal if we are on or off track. In addition to that, we will have continued assistance from our guides on the other side. On the real side.

The wounds we carry into lifetimes are open doors that let negative energy in and repeat patterns, but we can stop the patterns by having the courage to release the untruths that are trapped inside the wounds. Then the wounds can heal.

Untruths are the ego's interpretations of what happened. The ego, when untrained, is self-serving and will judge people and distort facts. We set ourselves free when we gather the courage to turn the ego's distortions into truths. Of course, it takes courage to overcome traumas, and we often prefer to remain in our thorny comfort zone, no matter how uncomfortable it is, because at least we know what the threats and our defenses are.

We fear the unknown even if we know that it may be better than what we have at present. But why wait longer? Remember the story of the Chinese lady who lost her love and remained fearful of seeing him again? Why wait longer, if you have wanted to find him again for so long?

The ego makes up all possible excuses to keep us jailed with monsters, bottled up with our own demons, while freedom is available at hand. We do not need a key. There is no door; there is no lock; there are no bars at the window. There are no walls either. There is only our willingness to say, "I choose differently."

Then the old, dark, heavy energy of suffering will begin to shift and change, as set by the Universal Law that nothing is destroyed. Instead, it will transform back into Light, and the lessons that were learned through those experiences shall be filed in the Akashic Records for reference.

I have to keep reminding myself that I need to be gentle with myself along the path of healing and transmuting the heavy energies. I tend to be impatient and would like to have permanent results immediately. That is why I get so frustrated when I fall again into traps and have relapses. I would like to make no more mistakes ever, but then I think that even the most experienced of concert players might play a false note once in a while.

What is sure is that I came into this lifetime equipped with the same courage that Black Jaguar had. I lived intensely, with no numbing, except the occasional help from herbs and chemical drugs to help me through dark nights of the soul, in addition to the unfailing comfort of the Ascended Masters.

I did live intensely through challenges and fears. I overcame the fear and anxiety of looking within me because some inner knowing, no matter how faint, kept me convinced that those fears, anxiety, daftness, and all the bad feelings and responses I experienced were not me. I knew that, even though the expression on the face of psychologists was not of total confidence. I was determined to find the true me beyond that tangle of briars.

No matter how much fear I experienced and sensed in this lifetime, I prayed to become fearless. I asked to be a soul who has gone through the dark illusions that I myself brought into being and to become strong and knowledgeable for the purpose of feeling comfortable and poised and able to help others who may still be wavering.

# Chapter 30

It is imperative for me to read this lifetime of mine through the eyes of Love if I want to change my future. But first of all, I must be clear on what Love is. Love with a capital L is a re-discovery of our true nature, our true essence, which comes from the Eternal Source of all creation: the Source of life eternal that underlies the transformations of energy at all its levels of appearance.

Love is a light, a shine, a glow permeating all fibers of my being, a knowing that Light itself is the truth of what we are. It expands from my heart, twinning its presence in other beings that it blesses with its sight, knowing that we are all in Oneness.

And since we are in Oneness, and we are energy, we need to be mindful of the energy of our thoughts because:

*To give and to receive are one in truth.*[1]

In other words, what you give, you give to yourself.

First of all, I claim responsibility for all that has happened to me, even if I do not remember when I made the decisions that have shaped this lifetime of mine.

However, I need not feel guilty for the bad things I have created—the

---

1. "Lesson 108: To Give and to Receive Are One in Truth". *A Course in Miracles*. https://acim.org/acim/lesson-108/to-give-and-to-receive-are-one-in-truth/en/s/512

hurt, the mistakes, even the violence—because all energy is part of the experiment to be acted out on Earth. Every baddie I encountered was the product of trial-and-error interactions between me and the other soul with whom I had to iron things out.

What is important is to reawaken to the thought of our true essence and reality, and finally tell ourselves that it is no longer necessary to play this game of acting characters that are fictitious and unhappy. Out of that view of the world, the forgiveness as intended in ACIM will emerge as an idea that is so much easier to adopt than the kind of forgiveness that religious tradition has taught.

Forgiving someone who has hurt us will, indeed, take time. However, that time will be shorter if I view the "baddie" as someone with whom I had a bump contract with and that the contract entailed its acting out on the stage of life. From that moment on, I can change my life.

I still do not love my mother, and I do not feel guilty about it. It will take me some more time, more energy to work through, to get there, especially about loving myself. But I am fully aware that we love each other very much indeed at the spiritual level. That is why we agreed to have such a hell of a time on Earth, again and again. Maybe I wouldn't have done it with anyone else.

I have no difficulty seeing a flame of eternity, no matter how dim or bright, when I think of my mother and when I envision the desk of the pediatrician, a.k.a. the high priest. My body still carries energies that I need to transmute in order to open up my hold on those two souls. Fully forgiving means I let you go. And in letting you go, I know that I am free too—finally fully free.

My mother is not here to defend herself from what I have written about her. I am sure she would have listed a lot of episodes and features of my personality that hurt her all her life. But that is not necessary to know here.

I am writing from the viewpoint of my own perception. My perception is composed of all the experiences I had before this incarnation and all the commas in the contracts that I agreed upon with many other souls to experience in this lifetime. I am the hub around which the energies that I carry in my whole electromagnetic field project out the reality that I create subconsciously. I perceive that reality in the way I am until I choose consciously to think, and therefore create, differently.

It is my choice to step out of illusions and return to Love steadily. I bless time for its presence. Although it is an illusion because it does not exist in eternity, which is reality, time accompanies our gentle, gradual transmutation of low-frequencies into higher frequencies, thus allowing the release of ideas and beliefs that no longer serve us.

Healing is an ongoing process as is forgiveness.

In processing the life of Black Jaguar and this lifetime of mine, I have become aware of how I do not love myself. I have always been demanding, stern, and critical about what I have done or not done and had to be exceedingly careful at how I proceeded and said things so as to keep self-criticism and the ever-lurking feeling of embarrassment to a minimum. I walked on eggshells all my life, keeping emotions repressed within me. Living life like that has caused me an inordinate amount of fatigue, which has kept me permanently in the red in my account of energy.

Keeping up the good work has made me feel safe enough to release, bit by bit, the heavy energies that weighed me down until I could see the ultimate underlying belief that kept me from loving myself. When Black Jaguar was castrated, he became convinced that no one could ever love him. He had lost one of the attributes of the warrior forever. A tribesman who is sexually impotent is useless and cannot be loved ever again.

But there was a girl, with bright, deep eyes, who never declared her admiration toward him and whose friendly love could not ever be stopped. When Black Jaguar and I became aware of the existence of that girl and her feelings, we realized that he had been loved all along, no matter what. And when I felt Black Jaguar's realization in my heart, I knew that I could be lovable, too.

Flipping the belief from "I am unlovable" to "I am lovable" has shone a bright light that has dispelled darkness within myself.

Now I can truly start a new chapter in my life.

I have reached an age at which I am proud to call myself a crone. I am proud of the wisdom I have gleaned throughout my life that has made me entitled to claim such a designation for myself. The crones of old were laden with years of experience of human behavior and knowledge of souls' illnesses and ways of healing them.

May I offer my own healing light, streaming from the core of my own wounded healer—my jaguar heart.

# *Acknowledgments*

I wish to thank first and foremost my husband, John, for teaching me joy and for the patience and support he has demonstrated all his life toward me and my healing path.

My gratitude goes to Doreen Reily and Karen LaGrange, whose open senses have relayed to me notions of my true mission in life, thus encouraging me to pursue a sacred path that would give purpose to my life and benefit others.

My heart sends gratitude to the Internet for enabling me to connect with kindred spirits all over the world, whom I embrace all in one loving hug. Some of these kindred spirits I have met in person in gatherings that they organized, thus allowing me to experience the power of groups, which is always greater than the sum of their parts. Some others I have listened to on podcasts or interviews and taken advantage of the sacred moments of meditation and healing they offered while on air, thus leading me to step forward along my path of healing, happiness, and freedom.

I am grateful to my editor, Sigrid Macdonald, for her skilled and loving guidance in advising me on how to fine-tune my text and thoughts, as well as for her appreciation of my first effort and encouragement to keep on writing.

# Bibliographical References

*A Course in Miracles*, Combined Volume (Third Edition) copyrighted © 2007 by the Foundation for Inner Peace, www.acim.org

Crowley, A., *Thoth Tarot Deck Standard*, US Games.

Harris, J.R., *The Nurture Assumption: Why Children Turn Out the Way They Do*. Free Press, New York, NY, 1998.

Yen Mah, A., *Falling Leaves*. Penguin, Harmondsworth, 2001.

# *About the Author*

**Anna Dodds** was born and raised in a traditional and religious society in Northern Italy, in which women's roles were clearly defined. While studying languages at the Interpreters' School of her local university, she met and later married her husband John. Anna is fluent in Italian, English, and Spanish, with knowledge of French and Mandarin, and used her skills to help people understand each other and work together in a UN institution for nearly thirty years.

Anna has traveled the world extensively and visited many temples and sacred places, including Machu Picchu. She is passionate about and accomplished in singing, qigong, and tai chi chuan, in which she obtained a second duan black belt and a first-level instructor certificate. She also has a master diploma in the Energy Healing Facilitator (EHF) technique. Today, Anna lives in the peaceful Italian countryside, where she enjoys gardening and continues her spiritual journey. *Jaguar Heart* is her first book.

Printed in the USA
CPSIA information can be obtained
at www.ICGtesting.com
CBHW031948090824
12961CB00013B/630